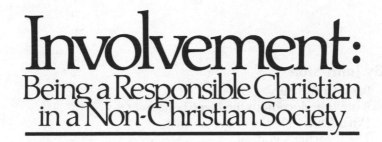

Involvement:
Being a Responsible Christian in a Non-Christian Society

By John Stott

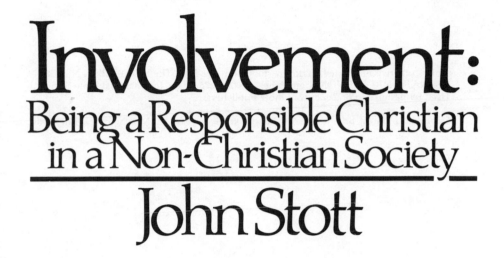

Involvement:
Being a Responsible Christian in a Non-Christian Society
John Stott

A Crucial Questions Book

Fleming H. Revell Company
Old Tappan, New Jersey

Published in Great Britain as *Issues Facing Christians Today* by Marshall Pickering, Ltd.

Library of Congress Cataloging in Publication Data

Stott, John R. W.
  Involvement.

  Bibliography: p.
  Includes index.
    1. Christian life—1960—   .   2. Church and
social problems.   3. Evangelicalism.   I. Title.
BV4501.2.S789   1985   261.8   84-24826
ISBN 0-8007-1418-0

Publisher's Foreword

IN A WORLD THAT HAS BECOME AN INTERRELATED GLOBAL VILLAGE of 4.5 billion men, women, and children, the problems of human existence have reached crisis proportions. Modern man stretches to achieve new heights, but his very advances in technological and scientific realms sometime threaten him with the loss of life's most precious gifts—and even life itself. In the midst of the crises, Christians believe the possibility for unprecedented good, for the flourishing of freedom, and for peace exists. This hopeful outlook is itself possible in a violent, threatened world because the Christian views the world from the center point of history, the Cross, where God dealt redemptively with the crux of the human problem.

While the Christian does not doubt God's ability nor His final victory, he struggles to know and to implement God's plan. Thankfully, there is an ongoing discussion of contemporary problems as Christians wrestle with agendas for action. As the publisher of the Crucial Questions series, we earnestly hope that these volumes will contribute positively to that discussion. Although the viewpoints expressed by the authors in this series may not always be those of the publisher, we are grateful for the opportunity to present them to the public, and we trust that these volumes will serve to stimulate Christians to fulfill their role as salt and light in today's world.

Contents

Part Two   Global Issues

Abbreviations

THE BIBLICAL TEXT QUOTED IS NORMALLY THAT OF THE NEW International Version. If another text is used, this is stated.

Arndt-Gingrich *A Greek-English Lexicon of the New Testament and Other Early Christian Literature* by William F. Arndt and F. Wilbur Gingrich (University of Chicago Press and Cambridge University Press, 1957).

AV   The Authorised (King James') Version of the Bible, 1611.

JB   The Jerusalem Bible (Darton, Longman and Todd, 1966).

NASB   The New American Standard Bible (Moody Press, Chicago, 1960).

NEB   The New English Bible (NT 1961, 2nd edition 1970; OT 1970).

NIV   The New International Version of the Bible (Hodder & Stoughton, NT 1974; OT 1979).

RSV   The Revised Standard Version of the Bible (NT 1946, 2nd edition 1971; OT 1952).

Introduction

ONE OF THE MOST NOTABLE FEATURES OF THE WORLDWIDE EVAN-
gelical movement during the last ten to fifteen years has been the
recovery of our temporarily mislaid social conscience. For approximately fifty years (c.1920–70) evangelicals were preoccupied with the task of defending the historic biblical faith against
the attacks of liberalism, and reacting against its 'social gospel.'
But now we are convinced that God has given us social as well as
evangelistic responsibilities in his world. Yet the half-century of
neglect has put us far behind in this area. We have a long way to
catch up.

*Involvement: Being A Responsible Christian in a Non-Christian So-
ciety* is my own contribution to the catching-up process. (A second book follows immediately; in Great Britain these are both
being published as one volume, *Issues Facing Christians Today*). Its
source may be traced to 1978/9, when Michael Baughen, now
Bishop of Chester, but then Rector of All Souls, invited me to
preach a series of occasional sermons under the title 'Issues Facing Britain Today.' Several of these chapters began their life in
the pulpit, and subsequently grew into lectures at the London
Institute for Contemporary Christianity, whose *raison d'être* is to
help people develop a Christian perspective on the complexities
of the modern world.

I confess that several times in the course of writing I have been
tempted to give up. I have felt now foolish and now presumptu-
ous to attempt such an undertaking. For I am in no sense a specialist in moral theology or social ethics, and I have no particular

expertise or experience in some of the fields into which I trespass. Moreover, each topic is complex, has attracted an extensive literature, only some of which I have been able to read, and is potentially divisive, even in a few cases explosive. Yet I have persevered, mainly because what I am venturing to offer the public is not a polished professional piece but the rough-hewn amateur work of an ordinary Christian who is struggling to think Christianly, that is, to apply the biblical revelation to the pressing issues of the day.

For this is my concern. I begin with a commitment to the Bible as 'God's Word written,' which is how it is described in the Anglican Articles and has been received by nearly all churches until comparatively recent times. Such is the basic presupposition of this book; it is not part of my present purpose to argue it. But Christians have a second commitment, namely to the world in which God has placed us. And our two commitments often seem to be in conflict. Being a collection of documents which relate to particular and distant events, the Bible has an archaic feel. It seems incompatible with our western culture, its space probes and microprocessors. Like every other Christian I feel myself caught in the painful tension between these two worlds. They are centuries apart. Yet I have sought to resist the temptation to withdraw from either world by capitulation to the other.

Some Christians, anxious above all to be faithful to the revelation of God without compromise, ignore the challenges of the modern world and live in the past. Others, anxious to respond to the world around them, trim and twist God's revelation in their search for relevance. I have struggled to avoid both traps. For the Christian is at liberty to surrender neither to antiquity nor to modernity. Instead, I have sought with integrity to submit to the revelation of yesterday within the realities of today. It is not easy to combine loyalty to the past with sensitivity to the present. Yet this is our Christian calling: to live under the Word in the world.

Many people have helped me develop my thinking. I thank the 'apostolic succession' of my Study Assistants—Roy McCloughry, Tom Cooper, Mark Labberton, Steve Ingraham, and Bob Wismer—who have compiled bibliographies, assembled groups for the discussion of sermon topics, gathered information and checked references. Bob Wismer has been specially helpful in the final stages, having read the manuscript twice and made valuable suggestions. So has Frances Whitehead, my secretary for twenty-eight years, in addition to typing the manuscript, which has been shared by Vivienne Curry. Steve Andrews, my present study assistant, has been meticulous in proof correcting. I also thank friends who have read different chapters and given me the benefit of their comments—Oliver Barclay, Raymond Johnston, John Gladwin, Mark Stephens, Roy McCloughry, Myra Chave-Jones and my colleagues at the London Institute— Andrew Kirk (Associate Director) and Martyn Eden (Dean). I am particularly grateful to Jim Houston, founding Principal and now Chancellor of Regent College, Vancouver, whose vision of the need for Christians to have an integrated world view has stimulated both my own thinking and the founding of the London Institute.

JOHN STOTT
June 1984

Part I

Christians in a Non-Christian Society

Chapter One

Involvement: Is It Our Concern?

IT IS EXCEEDINGLY STRANGE THAT ANY FOLLOWERS OF JESUS CHRIST should ever have needed to ask whether social involvement was their concern, and that controversy should have blown up over the relationship between evangelism and social responsibility. For it is evident that in his public ministry Jesus both 'went about . . . teaching . . . and preaching' (Matthew 4.23; 9.35 RSV) and 'went about doing good and healing' (Acts 10.38 RSV). In consequence, 'evangelism and social concern have been intimately related to one another throughout the history of the Church. . . . Christian people have often engaged in both activities quite unselfconsciously, without feeling any need to define what they were doing or why.'[1]

The Evangelical Heritage of Social Concern

There were some remarkable examples of this in eighteenth-century Europe and America. The Evangelical Revival, which stirred both continents, is not to be thought of only in terms of the preaching of the gospel and the converting of sinners to Christ; it also led to widespread philanthropy and profoundly affected society on both sides of the Atlantic. John Wesley remains the most striking instance. He is popularly remembered as the itinerant evangelist and open-air preacher. And so he was. But the gospel he preached inspired people to take up social

19

causes in the name of Christ. Historians have attributed to Wesley's influence rather than to any other the fact that Britain was spared the horrors of a bloody revolution like France's.

The change which came over Britain during this period was well documented in J. Wesley Bready's remarkable book *England Before and After Wesley*, subtitled 'The Evangelical Revival and Social Reform.' His research forced him to conclude that 'the true nursing-mother of the spirit and character values that have created and sustained Free Institutions throughout the English-speaking world,' indeed 'the moral watershed of Anglo-Saxon history,' was 'the much-neglected and oft-lampooned Evangelical Revival.'[2]

Bready described 'the deep savagery of much of the eighteenth century,'[3] which was characterised by 'the wanton torture of animals for sport, the bestial drunkenness of the populace, the inhuman traffic in African negroes, the kidnapping of fellow-countrymen for exportation and sale as slaves, the mortality of parish children, the universal gambling obsession, the savagery of the prison system and penal code, the welter of immorality, the prostitution of the theatre, the growing prevalence of lawlessness, superstition and lewdness; the political bribery and corruption, the ecclesiastical arrogance and truculence, the shallow pretensions of Deism, the insincerity and debasement rampant in Church and State—such manifestations suggest that the British people were then perhaps as deeply degraded and debauched, as any people in Christendom.'[4]

But then things began to change. And in the nineteenth century slavery and the slave trade were abolished, the prison system was humanised, conditions in factory and mine were improved, education became available to the poor, trades unions began, etc. etc.

'Whence, then, this pronounced humanity?—this passion for social justice, and sensitivity to human wrongs? There is but one answer commensurate with stubborn historical truth. It derived from a new social conscience. And if that social conscience, admittedly, was the offspring of more than one progenitor, it nonetheless was mothered and nurtured by the Evangelical Revival of vital, practical Christianity—a revival which illumined the central postulates of the New Testament ethic, which made real the Fatherhood of God and the Brotherhood of men, which pointed the priority of personality over property, and which directed heart, soul and mind, towards the establishment of the Kingdom of Righteousness on earth.'[5]

The Evangelical Revival 'did more to transfigure the moral character of the general populace, than any other movement British history can record.'[6] For Wesley was both a preacher of the gospel and a prophet of social righteousness. Wesley was 'the man who restored to a nation its soul.'[7]

The evangelical leaders of the next generation were committed with equal enthusiasm to evangelism and social action. The most famous among them were Granville Sharp, Thomas Clarkson, James Stephen, Zachary Macaulay, Charles Grant, John Shore (Lord Teignmouth), Thomas Babington, Henry Thornton, and of course their guiding light, William Wilberforce. Because several of them lived in Clapham, at that time a village three miles south of London, and belonged to Clapham Parish Church, whose Rector John Venn was one of them, they came to be known as 'the Clapham Sect,' although in Parliament and in the press they were mocked as 'the Saints.'

It was their concern over the plight of the African slaves which first brought them together. Three days before his death in 1791, John Wesley wrote to Wilberforce to assure him that God had raised him up for his 'glorious enterprise' and to urge him not to be weary of welldoing. It is largely to the Clapham Sect (under Wilberforce's leadership) that the credit belongs for the first settlement of freed slaves in Sierra Leone (1787), the abolition of the trade (1807), the registration of slaves in the colonies (1820), which put an end to slave smuggling, and finally their emancipation (1833). It is true that 'the Saints' were wealthy aristocrats, who shared some of the social blindspots of their time, but they were extremely generous in their philanthropy, and the range of their concerns was extraordinary. In addition to the slavery question, they involved themselves in penal and parliamentary reform, popular education (Sunday Schools, tracts and the *Christian Observer* newspaper), British obligation to its colonies (especially India), the spread of the gospel (they were instrumental in the founding of both the Bible Society and the Church Missionary Society), and factory legislation. They also campaigned against duelling, gambling, drunkenness, immorality, and cruel animal sports. And throughout they were directed and motivated by their strong evangelical faith.

Ernest Marshall Howse has written of them: 'This group of Clapham friends gradually became knit together in an astonishing intimacy and solidarity. They planned and laboured like a committee that never was dissolved. At the Clapham mansions they congregated by common impulse in what they chose to call their "Cabinet Councils" wherein they discussed the wrongs and injustices which were a reproach to their country, and the battles which would need to be fought to establish righteousness. And thereafter, in Parliament and out, they moved as one body, delegating to each man the work he could do best, that their common principles might be maintained and their common purposes be realized.'[8] Reginald Coupland in his biography of Wilberforce justly commented: 'It was, indeed, a unique phenomenon—this brotherhood of Christian politicians. There has never been anything like it since in British public life.'[9]

Anthony Ashley Cooper was elected to the British Parliament in 1826, aged twenty-five. First in the House of Commons, and then in the House of Lords as the seventh Earl of Shaftesbury, he concerned himself successively with the plight of lunatics, child workers in the factories and mills, 'climbing boys' or chimney sweeps, women and children in the mines, and the children of the slums, more than 30,000 of whom in London were without a home, and more than a million of whom in the whole country were without schooling. His biographer Georgina Battiscombe, who is often sharply critical of him, nevertheless concludes her account of his life with this generous tribute: 'No man has in fact ever done more to lessen the extent of human misery, or to add

to the sum total of human happiness.'[10] And he himself felt able
to claim that 'most of the great philanthropic movements of the
century have sprung from the Evangelicals.'[11]

The same story can be told of the United States in the last
century. Social involvement was both the child of evangelical religion and the twin sister of evangelism. This is clearly seen in
Charles G. Finney, who is best known as the lawyer turned
evangelist and author of *Lectures on Revivals of Religion* (1835).
Through his preaching of the gospel large numbers were brought
to faith in Christ. What is not so well known is that he was concerned for 'reforms' as well as 'revivals.' He was convinced, as
Donald W. Dayton has shown in his *Discovering an Evangelical
Heritage*, both that the gospel 'releases a mighty impulse toward
social reform' and that the church's neglect of social reform
grieved the Holy Spirit and hindered revival. It is astonishing to
read Finney's statement in his twenty-third lecture on revival
that 'the great business of the church is to reform the world. . . .
The Church of Christ was originally organised to be a body of
reformers. The very profession of Christianity implies the profession and virtually an oath to do all that can be done for the
universal reformation of the world.'[12]

It is hardly surprising to learn, therefore, that through Finney's
evangelism God raised up 'an army of young converts who became the troops of the reform movement of his age.' In particular, 'the anti-slavery forces . . . were drawn largely from the
converts of Finney's revivals.' Chief among these was Theodore
Weld who gave his whole life to the anti-slavery struggle. He was
converted under Finney's ministry and worked for a time as his
assistant.[13] Not that Weld was the American equivalent of Wilberforce, however, for he was not a parliamentarian. In fact, 'the
agitation (that is, the anti-slavery agitation in America) was accomplished not so much by heroes of reform as by very numerous obscure persons, prompted by an impulse religious in
character and evangelical in spirit, which began in the Great Revival of 1830.'[14]

The nineteenth century is known also for the enormous expansion of Christian missions which it witnessed. It must not be imagined, however, that the missionaries concentrated exclusively on preaching, or indeed that their social concern was restricted to aid and relief, to the neglect of development and even sociopolitical activity. It is doubtful if these distinctions have ever been neatly drawn in practice. The American missiologist Dr. R. Pierce Beaver has written: 'Social action in mission can be traced from the time of the apostles. . . . Concern was never limited to relief. The itinerating missionary carried with him a bag of medicines, new or better seed and plants, and improved livestock. Nevins introduced the modern orchard industry into Shantung. The Basel missionaries revolutionised the economy of Ghana by introducing coffee and cocoa grown by families and individuals on their own land. James McKean transformed the life of Northern Thailand by eliminating its three major curses—smallpox, malaria, and leprosy. Wells and pure water often came through the help of missionaries. Industrial schools were stressed through the nineteenth century, and industries were established. . . .' In addition, 'the missionaries were constantly the protectors of the native peoples against exploitation and injustice by government and commercial companies. . . . They played a very important part in the abolishing of forced labor in the Congo. They resisted blackbirding in the South Pacific. They fought fiercely for human rights in combating opium, foot-binding, and exposure of girl babies in China. They waged war against widow-burning, infanticide, and temple prostitution in India, and above all broke the social and economic slavery of the caste system for the low and outcaste peoples. . . .'[15]

Reasons for 'The Great Reversal'

So it seems to be an established fact that at least during the last century, not only in Britain and America but also through the agency of missionaries in Africa and Asia, the gospel of Jesus Christ produced the good fruit of social reform. But then something happened, especially among evangelical Christians. At some point during the first thirty years of this century, and especially during the decade following World War I, a major shift took place which the American historian Timothy L. Smith has termed 'The Great Reversal,' and which David O. Moberg investigates in his book with that title. Although Dr. Moberg does not attempt a thorough analysis of the origins of the evangelical renunciation of social responsibility, they seem to have included the following.

The first cause was a reaction against theological liberalism, which at the turn of the century was seeping into the churches of Europe and America. Evangelicals felt they had their backs to the wall. Understandably, they became preoccupied with the defence and proclamation of the gospel, for nobody else seemed to be championing historic, biblical Christianity. This was the period (actually 1910–15) when the series of twelve small books entitled *The Fundamentals* were published in the United States, from which the term 'fundamentalism' arose. When evangelicals were busy seeking to vindicate the fundamentals of the faith, they felt they had no time for social concerns.

Secondly, evangelicals reacted against the so-called 'social gospel' which theological liberals were developing at this time. Its most popular spokesman was Walter Rauschenbusch, who was Professor of Church History at Rochester Seminary, New York, from 1897 to 1917. He had come face-to-face with oppressive poverty during his twelve-year Baptist pastorate in New York City (1886–97), and this experience shaped his message.

In his first book *Christianity and the Social Crisis* (1907),[16] after tracing the social compassion of the Hebrew prophets, Jesus, and the early church, he criticised capitalism and advocated a simple kind of 'communism' or Christian socialism.[17] He also contrasted 'the old evangel of the saved soul' with 'the new evangel of the Kingdom of God.'[18] 'It is not a matter of getting individuals into heaven,' he wrote, 'but of transforming the life on earth into the harmony of heaven.'[19] Again, the 'essential purpose of Christianity' is 'to transform human society into the Kingdom of God by regenerating all human relationships.'[20] These quotations are enough to disclose his two errors, which led evangelicals to condemn the 'social gospel' and so hindered the development of an evangelical social programme. First, he identified the Kingdom of God with 'a reconstruction of society on a Christian basis.'[21] Secondly, he implied that human beings can establish the divine Kingdom by themselves (whereas Jesus always spoke of it as a gift of God). Though he said he cherished 'no Utopian delusion,'[22] he yet believed that 'it rests upon us to decide if a new era is to dawn in the transformation of the world into the Kingdom of God.'[23] The 'common aim' of church and state, he affirmed, 'is to transform humanity into the Kingdom of God.'[24]

It will be clear from this unguarded language that *Christianity and the Social Crisis* was not a work of serious theology. Nor was Rauschenbusch's second book, with its misleading title *Christianizing the Social Order* (1912). His third book gave the game away, however: *A Theology for the Social Gospel* (1917).[25] He began it with these ingenuous words: 'We have a social gospel. We need a systematic theology large enough to match it and vital enough to back it.' Indeed a 'readjustment and expansion of theology' is necessary in order to 'furnish an adequate intellectual basis for the social gospel.'[26] Thus Rauschenbusch betrayed himself. First, we formulate our social gospel, and only then do we hunt round for an intellectual or theological justification for it! He finds it in the Kingdom of God. 'This doctrine is itself the social gospel.'[27] For 'the Kingdom of God is humanity organized according to the will of God.'[28] 'The Kingdom of God is the Christian transfiguration of the social order.'[29]

But the Kingdom of God is not Christianised society. It is the divine rule in the lives of those who acknowledge Christ. It has to be 'received,' 'entered' or 'inherited,' Jesus said, by humble and penitent faith in him. And without a new birth it is impossible to see it, let alone enter it. Those who do receive it like a child, however, find themselves members of the new community of the Messiah, which is called to exhibit the ideals of his rule in the world and so to present the world with an alternative social reality. This social challenge of the gospel of the Kingdom is quite different from the 'social gospel.' When Rauschenbusch politicised the Kingdom of God, it is understandable (if regrettable) that, in reaction to him, evangelicals concentrated on evangelism and personal philanthropy, and steered clear of sociopolitical action.

The third reason for the evangelical neglect of social responsibility is the widespread disillusion and pessimism which followed World War I, because of its exposure of human evil. Earlier social programmes had failed. Man and his society appeared to be irreformable. Attempts at reform were useless. To be sure, because of the biblical doctrines of original sin and human depravity, evangelicals should not have been taken by surprise. But between the wars there was no evangelical leader to articulate the providence and common grace of God as grounds for persevering hope. Historic reformed Christianity was in eclipse.

Fourthly, there was the spread (specially through J. N. Darby's teaching and its popularisation in the Scofield Bible) of the premillennial scheme. This portrays the present evil world as beyond improvement or redemption, and predicts instead that it will deteriorate steadily until the coming of Jesus, who will then set up his millennial reign on earth. If the world is getting worse, and if only Jesus at his coming will put it right, the argument runs, there seems no point in trying to reform it meanwhile.

The fifth reason for evangelical alienation from social concern was probably the spread of Christianity among middle-class people, who tended to dilute it by identifying it with their own culture. This is without doubt one of the factors underlying the American sociological findings reported by Milton Rokeach in 1969 and summarised by David O. Moberg. These were highly critical of the negative social influences of organised religion. 'The general picture that emerges from the results presented . . . is that those who place a high value on *salvation* are conservative, anxious to maintain the *status quo*, and unsympathetic or indifferent to the plight of the black and the poor. . . . Considered all together, the data suggest a portrait of the religious-minded as a person having a self-centred preoccupation with saving his own soul, an other-worldly orientation, coupled with an indifference toward or even a tacit endorsement of a social system that would perpetuate social inequality and injustice.'

David Moberg tells how this report brought a storm of protest on the ground that the research methodology was faulty, but he adds that altogether to ignore these findings and conclusions 'would be a serious mistake.'[30] Although I have been able earlier to mention some fine examples of social action in the eighteenth and nineteenth centuries, there have certainly been other situations in which the church has acquiesced in oppression and exploitation, and has taken no action against these evils, nor even protested against them.

The 'great reversal' is explicable for these five reasons. We do not blame our evangelical forebears; in their place we would probably have reacted to contemporary pressures as they did. Not that all evangelicals mislaid their social conscience at the beginning of this century and between the wars. Some soldiered on, deeply involved in social as well as evangelistic ministries, and thus retained this indispensable outworking of the gospel, without which evangelicalism loses part of its authenticity. But most turned away. Then during the 1960s, the decade of protest, when young people were rebelling against the materialism, superficiality, and hypocrisy of the adult world they had inherited, the evangelical mainstream recovered its morale, and the process of 'Reversing the Great Reversal' (as David Moberg entitles his final chapter) got under way.

Probably the first voice to recall the evangelical constituency to its social responsibilities was that of the American Christian scholar Carl F. H. Henry, the founding editor of *Christianity Today*, in his book *The Uneasy Conscience of Modern Fundamentalism* (1947). Not many seemed to listen. But gradually the message caught on. And in 1966, at the conclusion of an American conference on world missions, the participants unanimously adopted the 'Wheaton Declaration' which firmly bracketed 'the primacy of preaching the gospel to every creature' and 'a verbal witness to Jesus Christ' with 'evangelical social action,' and urged 'all evangelicals to stand openly and firmly for racial equality, human freedom, and all forms of social justice throughout the world.'

In Britain in the early sixties a number of evangelical leaders began to grapple with the social application of the gospel. Most of them were laymen in professional and business life, and prominent among them was Professor Norman Anderson. Then in 1961 George Goyder's *The Responsible Company* was published, and in 1964 Fred Catherwood's *The Christian in Industrial Society*. This incipient groundswell of social concern found public expression at the first National Evangelical Anglican Congress at Keele University in 1967. There Anglican evangelicals publicly repented of their tendency to withdraw from both the secular world and the wider church, and committed themselves to conscientious involvement in both. As for the scope of mission, the Report says that 'evangelism and compassionate service belong together in the mission of God.'[31]

The turning point for the worldwide evangelical constituency was doubtless the International Congress on World Evangelisation held in July 1974 at Lausanne, Switzerland. Some 2,700 participants gathered from more than 150 nations under the slogan 'Let the Earth Hear His Voice,' and at the conclusion of the Congress endorsed the Lausanne Covenant. After three introductory sections on the purpose of God, the authority of the Bible, and the uniqueness of Christ, its fourth is entitled 'The Nature of Evangelism' and its fifth, 'Christian Social Responsibility.' The latter declares that 'evangelism and sociopolitical involvement are both part of our Christian duty.' But the two paragraphs stand side by side in the Covenant, with no attempt to relate them, except for the statement in paragraph 6 that 'in the church's mission of sacrificial service evangelism is primary.'

During the years which followed the Lausanne Congress there was a certain amount of tension within the evangelical movement, as some emphasised evangelism, others social activity, and all of us wondered how according to Scripture we should spell out the relationship between the two. So in June 1982, under the joint sponsorship of the Lausanne Committee and the World

Evangelical Fellowship, the 'Consultation on the Relationship between Evangelism and Social Responsibility' (CRESR) was held in Grand Rapids, and issued its report entitled *Evangelism and Social Responsibility: An Evangelical Commitment.* Although of course we did not see eye to eye on every point, God led us to a remarkable degree of consensus. Social activity was said to be both a consequence of and a bridge to evangelism, and indeed the two were declared to be partners. Besides, they are united by the gospel. 'For the gospel is the root, of which both evangelism and social responsibility are the fruits.'[32] The Report also has a chapter on 'History and Eschatology' and a final more practical chapter entitled 'Guidelines for Action.'

The Church and Politics

It will have been noted that the Lausanne Covenant speaks not just of 'social responsibility' but of 'sociopolitical involvement.' It is the use of the word 'political' which causes red warning lights to flash in the minds of many evangelicals. They have always engaged in humanitarian work, especially in medical and educational programmes; it is political activity of which they have often fought shy. Indeed, opposition to it is much wider than the evangelical constituency. Whenever the church (or any branch of it) becomes politically embroiled, a howl of protest can be expected from both within its membership and from outside. 'The church should steer clear of politics,' people cry. And 'religion and politics don't mix.'

Several different issues are involved in this controversy, and the waters of the debate are muddied by a failure to distinguish between them. The first is the definition of the word 'politics.' The second concerns the relation between the social and the political, and why they cannot be kept apart. Thirdly, we need to consider the reasons why some people oppose the church's involvement in politics, and what it is they are trying to safeguard. Then fourthly we need to ask to whom Christian political responsibility belongs.

First, we must define our terms. The words 'politics' and 'political' may be given either a broad or a narrow definition. Broadly

speaking, 'politics' denotes the life of the city (*polis*) and the responsibilities of the citizen (*politēs*). It is concerned therefore with the whole of our life in human society. Politics is the art of living together in community. According to its narrow definition, however, politics is the science of government. It is concerned with the development and adoption of specific policies with a view to their being enshrined in legislation.

Once this distinction is clear, we may ask whether Jesus was involved in politics. In the latter and narrower sense, he clearly was not. He never formed a political party, adopted a political programme or organised a political protest. He took no steps to influence the policies of Caesar, Pilate or Herod. On the contrary, he renounced a political career. In the other and broader sense of the word, however, his whole ministry was political. For he had himself come into the world, in order to share in the life of the human community, and he sent his followers into the world to do the same. Moreover, the Kingdom of God he proclaimed and inaugurated was a radically new and different social organisation, whose values and standards challenged those of the old and fallen community. In this way his teaching had 'political' implications. It offered an alternative to the status quo. His kingship, moreover, was perceived as a challenge to Caesar's, and he was therefore accused of sedition.

Secondly, we need to consider the relation between the 'social' and the 'political,' now using this word in its narrower sense. In its final chapter the *Grand Rapids Report* addressed itself to this question. It distinguished between 'social service' and 'social action,' and helpfully drew up the following table:

Social Service	Social Action
Relieving human need	Removing the causes of human need
Philanthropic activity	Political and economic activity
Seeking to minister to individuals and families	Seeking to transform the structures of society
Works of mercy	The quest for justice[33]

The Report went on to delineate sociopolitical action in these terms: 'It looks beyond persons to structures, beyond the rehabilitation of prison inmates to the reform of the prison system, beyond improving factory conditions to securing a more participatory role for the workers, beyond caring for the poor to improving—and when necessary transforming—the economic system (whatever it may be) and the political system (again, whatever it may be), until it facilitates their liberation from poverty and oppression.'[34]

It seems clear, then, that genuine Christian social concern will embrace both social service and social action. It would be very artificial to divorce them. Some cases of need cannot be relieved at all without political action (the harsh treatment of slaves could be ameliorated, but not slavery itself; it had to be abolished). To go on relieving other needs, though necessary, may condone the situation which causes them. If travellers on the Jerusalem-Jericho road were habitually beaten up, and habitually cared for by Good Samaritans, the need for better laws to eliminate armed robbery might well be overlooked. If road accidents keep occurring at a particular crossroads, it is not more ambulances that are needed, but the installation of traffic lights to prevent accidents. It is always good to feed the hungry; it is better if possible to eradicate the causes of hunger. So if we truly love our neighbours, and want to serve them, our service may oblige us to take (or solicit) political action on their behalf.

Why, then, is there so much hostility to the idea of the church becoming politically involved? This is our third question. Probably the most articulate recent criticism was launched by Dr. Edward Norman in his 1978 Reith Lectures *Christianity and the World Order*.[35] He was not actually denying either that 'biblical teachings have social consequences' ('they obviously do,' he said, p. 74), or that the love of God will involve Christians in 'corporate social and political action' (p. 79). His concern was rather over 'the politicization of Christianity,' by which he meant 'the internal transformation of the faith itself, so that it comes to be defined in terms of political values' and its essence is 'reinterpreted as a scheme of social and political action' (p. 2). Dr. Norman was surely right that Christianity cannot be reduced to or identified with a political programme. But it seems to me that he over-reacted to this tendency and so gave many people the impression that he thought the church should be entirely apolitical.

Yet the 1978 Reith Lectures contained at least four warnings, to which we will be wise to give heed, albeit critically. I will collate them in my own way:

1. The contemporary church's political *emphasis* eclipses what should be its central concerns, namely the individual ('personal redemption,' p. 78), the inward ('the indwelling Christ,' pp. 72–85) and the eternal ('the ethereal qualities of immortality,' p. 2). Dr. Norman is right that *some* churches have lost these dimensions altogether. Yet in retaining them, the church must not overlook its corporate, external, and temporal responsibilites. Christians are citizens of two kingdoms and have responsibilities in both. To love God with all our being is indeed the 'first and greatest' commandment; but to love our neighbour as ourselves is 'similar.' Each is askew without the other.

2. The contemporary church's political *opinions* are nothing but 'the moral and political idealism of the surrounding culture' (p. 32), whether this is western bourgeois liberalism or Marxism. All the church does is 'tag along, offering a religious gloss' to borrowed ideas (p. 4). It conforms, instead of criticising.

3. The contemporary church's political *contribution* is amateurish; it lacks the necessary expertise to participate.

4. The contemporary church's political *expectations* are naive, because it tends to forget human fallibility and sin.

It will be observed that all four criticisms are levelled at the particular behaviour of *some* churches (though Dr. Norman tends to generalise), and not at the concept itself that the Christian church does have sociopolitical responsibilities.

To whom do these responsibilities belong? That is our fourth and last question. Failure to ask and answer it is one of the main reasons for the current confusion over Christian political involvement. We need to distinguish between Christian individuals, groups, and churches. All individual Christians should be politically active in the sense that, as conscientious citizens, they will vote in elections, inform themselves about contemporary issues, share in the public debate, and perhaps write to a newspaper, lobby their member of parliament or take part in a demonstration. Further, some individuals are called by God to give their lives to political service, in either local or national government. Christians who share particular moral and social concerns should be encouraged to form or join groups which will study issues at a deeper level and take appropriate action. In some cases these will be exclusively Christian groups; in others, Christians will want to contribute their biblical perspective to mixed groups, whether in a political party, a trade union or a professional association.

Granted the propriety of political thought and action by Christian individuals and groups, however, should the church as church involve itself in politics? Certainly the church must teach both the law and the gospel of God. This is the duty of the church's pastors, teachers, and other leaders. And 'when the church concludes that biblical faith or righteousness requires it to take a public stand on some issue, then it must obey God's Word and trust him with the consequences' (*Grand Rapids Report*, p. 52). Whether we think the church should go beyond teaching and take corporate political action of some kind is likely to depend on whether we adhere to the Lutheran, Reformed or Anabaptist traditions within Protestantism in relation to church and state. At least we can agree that the church should not enter this field without the necessary expertise.

The Biblical Basis for Social Concern

What, then, is the biblical basis for social concern? Why should Christians get involved? In the end there are only two possible attitudes which Christians can adopt towards the world. One is escape and the other engagement. 'Escape' means turning our backs on the world in rejection, washing our hands of it (though finding with Pontius Pilate that the responsibility does not come off in the wash) and steeling our hearts against its agonised cries for help. In contrast, 'engagement' means turning our faces towards the world in compassion, getting our hands dirty, sore and worn in its service, and feeling deep within us the stirring of the love of God which cannot be contained.

Too many of us evangelicals either have been, or maybe still are, irresponsible escapists. Fellowship with each other in the church is more congenial than service in an apathetic and even hostile environment outside. Of course we make occasional evangelistic raids into enemy territory (that is our evangelical speciality); but then we withdraw again, across the moat, into our Christian castle (the security of our own evangelical fellowship), pull up the drawbridge, and even close our ears to the pleas of those who batter on the gate. As for social activity, we have tended to say that it is largely a waste of time in view of the imminent return of the Lord. After all, when the house is on fire, what is the point of hanging new curtains or rearranging the furniture? The only thing that we really should engage in is to rescue the perishing. Thus we have tried to salve our conscience with a bogus theology.

'Do you realise,' a coed student asked Tom Sine during one of his futurology seminars in the United States, 'if we start feeding hungry people, things won't get worse, and if things don't get worse, Jesus won't come?' She was utterly sincere, writes Tom Sine. He continues: 'The response of the coed . . . reflects what I call the Great Escape view of the future. . . . The irony of [this] approach to the future is that, while it claims to take God seriously, it unwittingly moves God outside history, insisting that even he is powerless "in these last days." . . . It unintentionally fashions him into an impotent absentee landlord, who has lost control of his world and of human history. . . . The Great Escape becomes an incredible copout from all Christ called us to be and to do.'[36]

Instead of seeking to evade our social responsibility, we need to open our ears and listen to the voice of him who calls his people in every age to go out into the lost and lonely world (as he did), in order to live and love, to witness and serve, like him and for him. For that is 'mission.' Mission is our human response to the divine commission. It is a whole Christian life-style, including both evangelism and social responsibility, dominated by the conviction that Christ sends us out into the world as the Father sent him into the world, and that into the world we must therefore go—to live and serve, suffer and die for him.

Still, however, we come back to the question 'why?' Why should Christians get involved in the world and its social problems? In reply, I propose to marshall five great doctrines of the Bible, which all of us already believe in theory, but which we tend to cut and trim in order to make them fit our escapist theology. My plea is that we have the courage to hold these doctrines in their biblical fulness. Any one of them should be sufficient to convince us of our Christian social responsibility; the five together leave us without excuse.

(1) A Fuller Doctrine of God

To begin with, we need a fuller doctrine of God. For we tend to forget that he is concerned for the whole of mankind and for the whole of human life in all its colour and complexity. These universals have important consequences for our thinking.

First, the living God is *the God of nature as well as of religion,* of the 'secular' as well as of the 'sacred.' In fact Christians are always uncomfortable about this distinction. For everything is 'sacred' in the sense that it belongs to God, and nothing is 'secular' in the sense that God is excluded from it. God made the physical universe, sustains it, and still pronounces it good (Genesis 1.31). Indeed, 'everything God created is good, and nothing is to be rejected if it is received with thanksgiving' (1 Timothy 4.4).

We should be more grateful than we usually are for the good gifts of a good Creator—for sex, marriage and the family, for the beauty and order of the natural world, for work and leisure, for friendships and the experience of interracial intercultural community, for music and other kinds of creative art which enrich the quality of human life. Our God is often too small because he

is too religious. We imagine that he is chiefly interested in religion—in religious buildings (churches and chapels), religious activities (worship and ritual) and religious books (Bibles and
Prayer Books). Of course he is concerned about these things, but
only if they are related to the whole of life. According to the Old
Testament prophets and the teaching of Jesus, God is very critical of 'religion,' if by that is meant religious services divorced
from real life, loving service, and the moral obedience of the
heart. 'Religion that God our Father accepts as pure and faultless
is this: to look after orphans and widows in their distress and to
keep oneself from being polluted by the world' (James 1.27). The
only value of religious services is that they concentrate into an
hour or so of public, vocal, congregational activity the devotion
of our whole life. If they do not do this, if instead we say and sing
things in church which have no corollary in our everyday life
outside church, at home and work, they are worse than worth-
less; their hypocrisy is positively nauseating to God.

Secondly, the living God is *the God of creation as well as of the
Covenant.* We Christians sometimes make the mistake which Israel made in the Old Testament when they concentrated exclusively on the God of the Covenant, who had chosen them out of
all the nations to be the holy nation, and who had pledged himself to them saying 'I will be your God and you shall be my people.' To be sure, this was a glorious truth. The notion of
'covenant' is a major biblical theme; the biblical revelation is unintelligible without it. But it is a dangerous half-truth. When Israel overemphasised it, they diminished the living God. They
reduced him to the status of a tribal deity, a petty godling. He
became Yahweh the god of the Israelites, more or less on a par
with Chemosh the god of the Moabites and Milcom the god of
the Ammonites. They also forgot the other nations, or simply
despised and rejected them.

But the Bible begins with the nations, not Israel; with Adam
not Abraham; with the creation not the Covenant. And when
God chose Israel, he did not lose interest in the nations.

Amos bravely gave voice to the word of the Lord: 'Are not you

Israelites the same to me as the Cushites [or Ethiopians]? . . . Did I not bring Israel up from Egypt, the Philistines from Caphtor [Crete] and the Arameans from Kir?' (Amos 9.7). Similarly, that arrogant emperor Nebuchadnezzar had to learn that 'the Most High is sovereign over the kingdoms of men and gives them to anyone he wishes' (Daniel 4.32). He rules over the nations. Their destiny is under his control. Although Satan is called 'the ruler of this world' and is *de facto* its usurper, God remains the ultimate governor of everything he has made. 'From heaven the LORD looks down and sees all mankind; from his dwelling place he watches all who live on earth—he who forms the hearts of all, who considers everything they do' (Psalms 33.13–15). More than that, he has promised that in blessing Abraham and his posterity he will bless all the families of the earth, and that one day he will restore what the fall has marred, and bring to perfection all that he has made.

Thirdly, the living God is *the God of justice as well as of justification*. Of course he is the God of justification, the Saviour of sinners, 'the compassionate and gracious God, slow to anger, abounding in love and faithfulness' (Exodus 34.6). But he is also concerned that our community life be characterised by justice.

> *He upholds the cause of the oppressed*
> *and gives food to the hungry.*
> *The LORD sets prisoners free,*
> *the LORD gives sight to the blind,*
> *The LORD lifts up those who are bowed down,*
> *the LORD loves the righteous.*
> *The LORD watches over the alien*
> *and sustains the fatherless and widow,*
> *but he frustrates the ways of the wicked.*
> *Psalms 146.7–9*

This does not mean that he does all these things invariably, but rather that this is the kind of God he is.

Moreover, God's concern for justice extends beyond his own to all people, although he expects it particularly among his own people. Social compassion and justice mattered in the nations as well as in Israel. There is no clearer evidence of this than in the first two chapters of the prophecy of Amos. Before Amos rebuked Judah for rejecting God's law and turning to idolatry, and Israel for crushing the poor and denying justice to the oppressed (2.4–8), he pronounced God's judgment on all the surrounding nations (1.3–2.3)—on Syria for savage cruelty, on Philistia for capturing whole communities and selling them into slavery, on Tyre for breaking a treaty of brotherhood and Edom for pitiless hostility to Israel, on Ammon for atrocities in warfare and Moab for desecrating the bones of a neighbouring king.

Several of the prophetic books similarly contain a section of oracles about or against the nations. That God is the God of justice, and desires justice in every nation and community, is particularly evident from the Book of Nahum, which is a prophecy against Nineveh, the capital and symbol of Assyria. Yahweh's denunciation of Assyria is not just because she was Israel's longstanding enemy (e.g. 1.9ff; 2.2ff), but because of her idolatry (1.14) and because she is a 'city of blood, full of lies, full of plunder, never without victims' (3.1). Twice Yahweh says the terrible words 'I am against you' (2.13; 3.5), and the oracle ends with the rhetorical question (3.19), 'who has not felt your endless cruelty?'

It is clear from these Old Testament passages that God hates injustice and oppression *everywhere*, and that he loves and promotes justice *everywhere*. Indeed wherever righteousness is to be found in our fallen world, it is due to the working of his grace. All human beings know this too. For we have an inbuilt sense of justice, to which the child's expostulation 'it isn't fair!' bears eloquent witness. It is solid evidence of Paul's teaching that God's moral law is written on the human heart (Romans 2.14, 15). Both God's law and God's gospel are for our good.

Here then is the living God of the Bible. His concerns are all-embracing—not only the 'sacred' but the 'secular,' not only religion but nature, not only his covenant people but all people, not only justification but social justice in every community, not only his gospel but his law. So we must not attempt to narrow down his interests. Moreover, ours should be as broad as his.

John Gladwin sums up this argument well in his *God's People in*

God's World: 'It is because this is God's world, and he cared for it to the point of incarnation and crucifixion, that we are inevitably committed to work for God's justice in the face of oppression, for God's truth in the face of lies and deceits, for service in the face of the abuse of power, for love in the face of selfishness, for cooperation in the face of destructive antagonism, and for reconciliation in the face of division and hostility.'[37]

(2) A Fuller Doctrine of Man

All our philanthropic work (that is, work inspired by love for man) depends on our evaluation of man. The higher our view of the worth of human beings, the more we shall want to serve them.

Secular humanists, who are sincere in describing themselves as dedicated to 'the human case and the human cause,'[38] sometimes appear more humane than Christians. But if we ask them why they are so committed to humankind, they are likely to reply with Julian Huxley that it is because of the human potential in the future aeons of evolution. 'Thus the development of man's vast potential of realizable possibility,' he wrote, 'provides the prime motive for collective action.'[39] The inadequacy of this as a basis for service is obvious. If the unimpeded progress of evolution were our chief concern, why should we care for the senile, the imbecile, the hardened criminal, the psychopath, the chronically sick, or the starving? Would it not be more prudent to put them to sleep like a well-loved dog, lest they hinder the evolutionary process? Compulsory euthanasia, not compassionate service, would be the logical deduction from the humanists' premise. The fact that they draw back from this abyss indicates that their heart is better than their head, and their philanthropy than their philosophy.

Christian people have a more sound basis for serving their fellow human beings. It is not because of what men may become in the speculative future development of the race, but because of what we already are by divine creation. Human beings are godlike beings, made in God's likeness, and possessing unique capacities which distinguish them from the animal creation. True, human beings are fallen, and the divine image is defaced, but despite all contrary appearances it has not been destroyed (Genesis 9.6; James 3.9). It is this which accounts for their unique worth and which has always inspired Christian philanthropy.

These human but godlike creatures are not just souls (that we should be concerned exclusively for their eternal salvation), nor just bodies (that we should care only for their food, clothing, shelter, and health), nor just social beings (that we should become entirely preoccupied with their community problems). They are all three. A human being might be defined from a biblical perspective as 'a body-soul-in-community.' That is how God has made us. So if we truly love our neighbours, and because of their worth desire to serve them, we shall be concerned for their total welfare, the wellbeing of their soul, body, and community. And our concern will lead to practical programmes of evangelism, relief, and development. We shall not just prattle and plan and pray, like that country vicar to whom a homeless woman turned for help, and who (doubtless sincerely, and because he was busy and felt helpless) promised to pray for her. She later wrote this poem and handed it to a regional officer of *Shelter*:

> I was hungry,
>   and you formed a humanities group to discuss my hunger.
> I was imprisoned,
>   and you crept off quietly to your chapel and prayed for my
>   release.
> I was naked,
>   and in your mind you debated the morality of my appearance.
> I was sick,
>   and you knelt and thanked God for your health.
> I was homeless,
>   and you preached to me of the spiritual shelter of the love of
>   God.
> I was lonely,
>   and you left me alone to pray for me.
> You seem so holy, so close to God
>   But I am still very hungry—and lonely—and cold.

Motivated by love for human beings in need, the early Christians went everywhere preaching the Word of God, because nothing has such a humanising influence as the gospel. Later they founded schools, hospitals, and refuges for the outcast. Later still they abolished the slave trade and freed the slaves, and they improved the conditions of workers in mills and mines, and of prisoners in gaols. They protected children from commercial exploitation in the factories of the West and from ritual prostitution in the temples of the East. Today they bring leprosy sufferers both the compassion of Jesus and modern methods of reconstructive surgery and rehabilitation. They care for the blind and the deaf, the orphaned and the widowed, the sick and the dying. They get alongside junkies, and stay alongside them during the traumatic period of withdrawal. They set themselves against racism and political oppression. They get involved in the urban scene, the inner city, the slums and the ghettoes, and raise their protest against the inhuman conditions in which so many are doomed to live. They seek in whatever way they can to express their solidarity with the poor and hungry, the deprived and the disadvantaged. I am not claiming that all Christians at all times have given their lives in such service. But a sufficiently large number have done so to make their record noteworthy.

Why have they done it? Because of the Christian doctrine of man—male and female, all made in the image of God, though all also fallen. Because people matter. Because every man, woman, and child has an intrinsic, inalienable value as a human being. Once we see this, we shall both set ourselves to liberate people from everything dehumanising and count it a privilege to serve them, to do everything in our power to make human life more human.

The film *The Elephant Man* has recently made widely known the extraordinary story with which every English person was familiar at the end of the last century. In 1884 Frederick Treves, a young surgeon and lecturer in anatomy at the London Hospital, found the Elephant Man in a rented shop opposite the hospital entrance. When Treves first saw his hunched-up form, he thought him 'the embodiment of loneliness.' He later described him as 'the most disgusting specimen of humanity' he had ever seen. He had an 'enormous, misshapen head,' with a huge bony mass projecting from his brow, and another from his upper jaw which gave him an elephantine appearance. Spongy, evil-smelling skin, like fungus or brown cauliflower, hung in bags from his back, chest, the back of his head and his right arm. His legs were deformed, his feet bulbous, and he had hip disease. His face was expressionless, and his speech spluttering, almost unintelligible. His left arm and hand, however, were as shapely and delicate as a young woman's.

To add to his suffering, he was treated like an animal, hawked from fair to fair, and exhibited to the curious for two pence a look. Treves wrote: 'He was shunned like a leper, housed like a wild beast, and got his only view of the world from a peephole in a showman's cart.' He received less kindness than a dog, and, terrified of staring eyes, he would creep into a dark corner to hide.

When he was abandoned by the circus showman, Treves had him accommodated and cared for in a room at the back of the London Hospital where three and a half years later he died in his sleep, a few days after he had received his Easter Day Communion.

Treves had imagined that he was an imbecile, probably from birth. But in the hospital he discovered that he was a human being, Joseph Merrick by name, in his early twenties, highly intelligent, a voracious reader, with a passion for conversation, an acute sensibility, and a romantic imagination. He was also a 'gentle, affectionate and lovable creature.'

When the first woman visited Joseph Merrick, gave him a smile and a greeting, and actually shook him by the hand, he broke down into uncontrollable sobbing. But from that day his transformation began. He became a celebrity, and many notable people visited him. Gradually he changed 'from a hunted thing into a man,' wrote Treves. But actually he had always been a man. Treves may never have articulated the Christian doctrine of human beings made in the image of God. Nevertheless, it was his remarkable respect for Joseph Merrick which enabled him to lift up his poor misshapen head, and gain some measure of self-respect before he died.[40]

(3) A Fuller Doctrine of Christ

There have been many different reinterpretations and reconstructions of Jesus. Indeed, it is right that every generation of Christians should seek to understand and to present him in terms appropriate to their own age and culture. So we have had Jesus the ascetic, the sufferer, the monarch, the gentleman, the clown, the superstar, the capitalist, the socialist, the revolutionary, the guerrilla, the wonder drug. Several of these portraits are mutually contradictory, of course, and others have little or no historical warrant.

We need then to recover an authentic picture of him whom the Lausanne Covenant calls 'the historical, biblical Christ' (para. 4). We need to see him in his paradoxical fulness—his sufferings and glory, his servanthood and lordship, his lowly Incarnation and cosmic reign. It is perhaps the Incarnation which we evangelicals have tended to neglect, in both its theological significance and its practical implications.

The Son of God did not stay in the safe immunity of his heaven. He emptied himself of his glory and humbled himself to serve. He became little, weak, and vulnerable. He entered into our pain, our alienation, and our temptations. He not only proclaimed the good news of the Kingdom of God, but demonstrated its arrival by healing the sick, feeding the hungry, forgiving the sinful, befriending the dropout, and raising the dead. He had not come to be served, he said, but to serve and to give his life as a ransom price for the release of others. So he allowed himself to become a victim of gross injustice in the courts, and as they crucified him he prayed for his enemies. Then in the awful God-forsaken darkness he bore our sins in his own innocent person.

Should not this vision of Christ affect our understanding of his commission, 'As the Father has sent me, I am sending you' (John 20.21)? For if the Christian mission is to be modelled on Christ's mission, it will surely involve for us, as it did for him, an entering into other people's worlds. In evangelism it will mean entering their thought world, and the world of their tragedy and lostness, in order to share Christ with them where they are. In social activity it will mean a willingness to renounce the comfort and security of our own cultural background in order to give ourselves in service to people of another culture, whose needs we may never before have known or experienced. Incarnational mission, whether evangelistic or social or both, necessitates a costly identification with people in their actual situations. Jesus of Nazareth was moved with compassion by the sight of needy human beings, whether sick or bereaved, hungry, harassed or helpless; should not his people's compassion be aroused by the same sights?

Leonidas Proaño is Roman Catholic bishop of Riobama, about a hundred miles south of Quito, Ecuador. Basing his thinking on the Bible, he is concerned for social justice in his country, not least for the Indians whose culture he wants to see preserved against those who threaten to erode and even destroy it. Although he refuses to identify himself with Marxism, and is in fact not a Marxist, he is critical—indeed defiant—of the political and ecclesiastical system in his country. He opposes feudalism and the oppressive power of the wealthy landowners. It is perhaps not surprising that there have been threats to assassinate him. At all events, after the overthrow and death in 1973 of President Salvador Allende of Chile, Bishop Proaño preached at a mass for Marxist students in Quito. He portrayed Jesus as the radical he was, the critic of the establishment, the champion of the downtrodden, the lover of the poor, who not only preached the gospel but also gave compassionate service to the needy. After the mass there was a question-time, during which some students said: 'If we had known *this* Jesus, we would never have become Marxists.'

Which Jesus do we believe in? And which Jesus do we preach?

Is it possible that in some parts of the church such a false Jesus ('another Jesus'—2 Corinthians 11.4) is being presented to the young people, that we are repelling them from him and driving them into the arms of Karl Marx instead?

(4) A Fuller Doctrine of Salvation

There is a constant tendency in the church to trivialise the nature of salvation, as if it meant no more than a self-reformation, or the forgiveness of our sins, or a personal passport to paradise, or a private mystical experience without social or moral consequences. It is urgent that we rescue salvation from these caricatures and recover the doctrine in its biblical fulness. For salvation is a radical transformation in three phases, beginning now, continuing throughout our earthly life and brought to perfection when Christ comes. In particular, we must overcome the temptation to separate truths which belong together.

First, *we must not separate salvation from the Kingdom of God.* In the Bible these two are virtually synonymous, alternative models to describe the same work of God. According to Isaiah 52.7 those who preach good news of peace are also those 'who proclaim salvation, who say to Zion, "Your God reigns!"' That is, where God reigns, he saves. Salvation is the blessing of his rule. Again, when Jesus said to his disciples 'how hard it is to enter the Kingdom of God,' it seems to have been natural for them to respond with the question, 'who then can be saved?' (Mark 10.24–26). They evidently equated entering the Kingdom with being saved.

Once this identification has been made, salvation takes on a broader aspect. For the Kingdom of God is God's dynamic rule, breaking into human history through Jesus, confronting, combating, and overcoming evil, spreading the wholeness of personal and communal wellbeing, taking possession of his people in total blessing and total demand. The church is meant to be the Kingdom community, a model of what human community looks like when it comes under the rule of God, and a challenging alternative to secular society. Entering God's Kingdom is entering the new age, long promised in the Old Testament, which is also the beginning of God's new creation. Now we look forward to the consummation of the Kingdom when our bodies, our society, and our universe will all be renewed, and sin, pain, futility, disease, and death will all be eradicated. Salvation is a big concept; we have no liberty to reduce it.

Secondly, *we must not separate Jesus the Saviour from Jesus the Lord.* It is little short of incredible that some evangelists teach the possibility of accepting Jesus as Saviour, while postponing a surrender to him as Lord. But God has exalted Jesus to his right hand and made him Lord. From that position of supreme power and executive authority he is able to bestow salvation and the gift of the Spirit. It is precisely because he is Lord that he can save. The affirmations 'Jesus is Lord' and 'Jesus is Saviour' are almost interchangeable. And his lordship extends far beyond the religious bit of our lives. It embraces the whole of our experience, public and private, home and work, church membership and civic duty, evangelistic and social responsibilities.

Thirdly, *we must not separate faith from love.* Evangelical Christians have always emphasised faith. *Sola fide,* 'by faith alone,' was one of the great watchwords of the Reformation, and rightly so. 'Justification,' or acceptance with God, is not by good works which we have done or could do; it is only by God's sheer unmerited favour ('grace'), on the sole ground of the atoning death of Jesus Christ, by simple trust in him alone. This central truth of the gospel cannot be compromised for anything.

But, although justification is by faith alone, this faith cannot remain alone. If it is living and authentic, it will inevitably issue in good works; and if it does not, it is spurious. Jesus himself taught this in his 'sheep and goats' description of Judgment Day. Our attitude to him, he said, will be revealed in, and so judged by, our good works of love to the least of his brothers and sisters. The apostles all lay the same emphasis on the necessity of good works of love. We all know that James taught it: 'faith by itself, if it is not accompanied by action, is dead. . . . I will show you my faith by what I do' (2.17, 18). So does John: 'If anyone has material possessions and sees his brother in need but has no pity on him, how can the love of God be in him?' (1 John 3.17). And so does Paul. Christ died to create a new community who would be 'eager to do what is good' (Titus 2.14). We have been recreated in Christ 'to do good works, which God prepared in advance for us to do' (Ephesians 2.10). Again, 'the only thing that counts is faith expressing itself through love. . . . Serve one another in love' (Galatians 5.6, 13). This, then, is the striking sequence—faith, love, service. True faith issues in love, and true love issues in service.

Specially those of us who are called 'evangelical' Christians need to take this New Testament emphasis to heart. We have to beware of magnifying faith and knowledge at the expense of love. Paul did not. If he were able to 'fathom all mysteries and all knowledge,' he wrote, and if he had 'a faith that can move mountains,' yet without love he would be nothing (1 Corinthians 13.2). For saving faith and serving love belong together. Whenever one is absent, so is the other. Neither can exist in isolation.

(5) A Fuller Doctrine of the Church

Many people think of the church as a kind of club, rather like the local golf club, except that the common interest of its members happens to be God rather than golf. They are religious people who do religious things together. They pay their subscription and are entitled to the privileges of club membership. In that frame of mind they forget William Temple's perceptive phrase that 'the church is the only cooperative society that exists for the benefit of nonmembers.'[41]

In place of the 'club' model of the church, we need to recover what could be described as the church's 'double identity.' On the one hand, the church is a 'holy' people, called out of the world to belong to God. But on the other it is a 'worldly' people, in the sense of being sent back into the world to witness and to serve. This is what Dr. Alec Vidler, following a lead of Bonhoeffer's, has called the church's 'holy worldliness.'[42]

Seldom in its long and chequered history has the church remembered or preserved its double identity. Sometimes, in a right emphasis on its 'holiness,' the church has wrongly withdrawn from the world and become insulated from it. At other times, in a right emphasis on its 'worldliness' (i.e. its immersion in the life of the world), the church has wrongly become assimilated to the world's standards and values, and so become contaminated by them. Yet without the preservation of both parts of its identity, the church cannot engage in mission. Mission arises out of the biblical doctrine of the church in society. An unbalanced ecclesiology makes mission unbalanced too.

Jesus taught these truths himself, not only in his famous 'in the world but not of it' expression, but in his vivid metaphors of the salt and the light. 'You are the salt of the earth,' he said, and 'you are the light of the world' (Matthew 5.13–16). He implied that the two communities, the new and the old, the church and the world, are as radically different from one another as light from darkness and salt from decay. He also implied that, if they were to do any good, the salt must soak into the meat, and the light must shine into the darkness. Just so, Christians must penetrate non-Christian society. Thus, the double identity and responsibility of the church are plain.

In a similar way the apostle Peter describes the members of God's new people on the one hand as 'aliens and strangers in the world' and on the other as needing to be conscientious citizens in it (1 Peter 2.11–17). We cannot be totally 'world-affirming' (as if nothing in it were evil), nor totally 'world-denying' (as if nothing in it were good), but a bit of both, and particularly 'world-challenging,' recognising its potentiality as God's world and seeking to conform its life increasingly to his lordship.

This vision of the church's influence on society is best described in terms of 'reform' rather than 'redemption.' As A. N. Triton has expressed it, 'Redemption is not an infection of social structures. . . . It results in individuals restored to a right relationship to God. But that sets up horizontal shock waves in society from which all of us benefit. These benefits are in terms of *reforming* society according to God's *law*, and not *redeeming* it by the death of Christ.'[43]

The effectiveness of the church depends on its combination of 'holiness' and 'worldliness.' We shall return to these images later.

Practical Action

I have assembled five doctrines and pleaded that we hold them in their biblical fulness—the doctrines of God (Creator, Lawgiver, Lord, and Judge), of human beings (their unique worth because made in God's image), of Christ (who identified with us and calls us to identify with others), of salvation (a radical transformation), and of the church (distinct from the world as its salt and light, yet penetrating it for Christ). These five doctrines constitute the biblical basis for mission, for both evangelistic and social responsibility. They lay upon us an obligation to be involved in the life of the world. But how?

Take the individual Christian first. In general terms, every Christian is called to be both a witness and a servant, for each of us is a follower of the Lord Jesus who both witnessed a good confession and said 'I am among you as a serving man.' Thus *diakonia* (service) and *marturia* (witness) are inseparable twins. Yet different Christians are called to different specialist ministries, just as the Twelve were called to the ministry of the Word and prayer, while the Seven were called to take charge of the daily distribution to the widows (Acts 6).

The metaphor of the church as the Body of Christ enforces the same lesson. Just as each member of the human body has a different function, so each member of the Body of Christ has a different gift and so a different ministry. At the same time, whatever our specialist calling may be, emergencies will override it. The priest and the Levite in the Parable of the Good Samaritan could not excuse their shameful neglect of the man, who had been assaulted and robbed, by saying that their calling was to work in the Temple. If we are called to a predominantly social ministry, we still have an obligation to witness. If we are called to a predominantly evangelistic ministry, we still cannot say we have no social responsibilities.

As for the local church, the versatility of its outreach can be greatly increased if full use is made of all its members with their different gifts and callings. It is a very healthy thing for the local church's oversight or leadership to encourage people with identical concerns to coalesce into 'special interest' groups or 'study and action' groups. Some will have an evangelistic objective—house-to-house visitation, a music group, a world mission group, etc. Other groups will have a social concern—sick and welfare visitors, a housing association, community or race relations, a pro-life, anti-abortion group, the needs of an ethnic minority, etc. Such specialist groups supplement one another. If an occasional opportunity is given to them to report back to the church membership as a whole, the representative nature of their work will be affirmed, and they can receive valuable support from their parent body in terms of advice, encouragement, prayer, and financial backing.

No one Christian could, or should try to, get involved in every kind of ministry. But each local church (at least of any size) can and should get involved in as many as possible, *through its groups.* The groups make it realistic for the church greatly to diversify its concern and action.

I end this chapter with what may be a rather surprising reference to the Roman Catholic mass. The word *mass* is said to be derived from the final sentence of the old Latin rite, *ite missa est.* In polite English it might be rendered 'now you are dismissed.' In more blunt language it could be just 'get out!'—out into the world which God made and God-like beings inhabit, the world into which Christ came and into which he now sends us. For that is where we belong. The world is the arena in which we are to live and love, witness and serve, suffer and die for Christ.

Chapter Two

Complexity: Can We Think Straight?

LET US SUPPOSE WE ARE AGREED THAT OUR DOCTRINES OF GOD AND man, of Christ, salvation and the church commit us inescapably to becoming socially involved—not only in social service, caring in Christ's name for the victims of oppression, but also in social action, concerned for justice and social change. To be thus strongly motivated is essential, but it is not enough. Any contribution we may hope to make will depend on our comprehension of the issues. We will be wise not to blunder unprepared into the minefield of social ethics. As I once heard the late John Mackay say, when he was President of Princeton Theological Seminary, 'Commitment without reflection is fanaticism in action, though reflection without commitment is the paralysis of all action.'

We should certainly not underestimate the complexity of the issues which confront mankind today. True, every generation has felt baffled by its contemporary problems; so it is not surprising that we should feel the same way. Yet the number, scale, and gravity of the questions facing us at the end of the twentieth century do seem to be unprecedented, owing particularly to the scientific revolution. For example, the problem of war and peace has always troubled the Christian conscience, but the development of nuclear weaponry has greatly aggravated it. Similarly, the new microtechnology has added to the problem of long-term unemployment, while the unravelling of the genetic code and the possibilities of genetic engineering have necessitated the new field of 'bioethics.'

Clearly no Christian can make himself an authority in all these areas, and it is also doubtful whether the church as such should be recommending particular and detailed policies. William Temple, who has certainly been the most socially concerned Archbishop of Canterbury this century, made much of the need to distinguish between principles and policies. Writing in 1941 of continuing poverty and malnutrition in Britain, and of 'the industrial life of the country . . . disgraced by chronic unemployment,' he went on: 'The Church is both entitled and obliged to condemn the society characterized by these evils; but it is not entitled in its corporate capacity to advocate specific remedies.'[1] Instead, the church should inspire its members (whether politicians, civil servants, businessmen, trade unionists or in other areas of public life) to seek and apply appropriate remedies. 'In other words, the Church lays down principles; the Christian citizen applies them; and to do this he utilizes the machinery of the State.'[2] Again, 'The Church cannot say how it is to be done; but it is called to say that it must be done.'[3]

The following year, in his better known book *Christianity and the Social Order*, Temple was still emphasising the same distinction. 'The Church is committed to the everlasting Gospel . . . ; it must never commit itself to an ephemeral programme of detailed action.'[4]

Readers of Temple will know that he was very far from saying that religion and politics do not mix. His point was different, namely that 'the Church is concerned with principles and not policy.'[5] The reasons why he believed the church as a whole should refrain from 'direct political action' by developing and advocating specific programmes could be summed up as 'integrity' (the church lacks the necessary expertise, though some of her members may have it), 'prudence' (because she may prove to be mistaken and so be discredited), and 'justice' (because different Christians hold different opinions, and the church should not side with even a majority of its members against an equally loyal minority).

Even if we agree with this clarification of roles, and concede that not all Christians are responsible for working out policies, we still have to grapple with the principles, and these are by no means always easy to formulate.

Some Christians in this situation give up in despair. 'The age-long problems such as war, economics, and divorce,' they say, 'have always divided Christians. There have always been pacifists and nonpacifists, capitalists and socialists, lax and rigid attitudes to divorce. And our modern problems, being more complex, are also more divisive. Besides,' they continue, 'there's no such thing as "the Christian view" on any of these problems; there is a whole spectrum of Christian views. Even the Bible does not always help us; it was written in such ancient cultures that it does not speak to our modern problems. So let us leave it to the experts and give up hope of finding a Christian answer ourselves.' Such despair denigrates God, because it denies the usefulness of his revelation as 'a lamp to [our] feet and a light for [our] path' (Psalms 119.105). To abandon hope of having anything Christian to say may even be mental laziness in the guise of a false humility.

True humility will lead us to sit patiently under the revelation of God and to affirm by faith that he can bring us to a substantially common mind. How can we believe in the Word and Spirit of God, and deny this? What is needed is more conscientious group study in which (1) we learn to pray together, (2) we listen attentively to each other's positions, and to the deep concerns which lie behind them, and (3) we help each other to discern the cultural prejudices which make us reluctant and even unable to open our minds to alternative viewpoints. This kind of discipline is painful, but Christian integrity demands it. As a result, we shall refuse to acquiesce in superficial polarisations, for the truth is always more subtle and sophisticated than that. Instead, we shall undertake some careful mapwork, plotting (and emphasising) areas of agreement, and clarifying residual disagreements with which we will continue perseveringly to wrestle.

If despair is one reaction to the complexity of modern ethical problems, its opposite is a naive over-simplification. Some Christians (particularly evangelical Christians, I fear) have tended to jump in head first. Either unwilling or unable to grasp the issues, we have sometimes denied that there are any. Or we have reasserted our evangelical watchword about the 'perspicuity' of Scripture, as if that meant there were no problems. We have then given glib answers to complex questions, and have treated the Bible as if it resembled either a slot machine (in goes your penny, out comes your answer) or that extraordinary Victorian almanac entitled 'Enquire Within,' which offered information on everything.

Certainly, the way of salvation is plain or 'perspicuous,' which is what the Reformers meant by the term. But how can we assert that Scripture contains no problems when the apostle Peter himself declared that in his brother apostle Paul's letters there were 'some things that are hard to understand' (2 Peter 3.16)? How to apply God's ancient word to the modern world is also hard. To deny this is another way of denigrating God, this time because it misunderstands the nature of his self-revelation.

Thus, to assert that there are no solutions and to offer slick solutions are both dishonouring to God. For on the one hand he *has* revealed his will to us, and on the other he has *not* revealed it in a set of neat propositions.

A Christian Mind

There is a third, better and more Christian way to approach today's complicated questions: develop a Christian mind, namely a mind which has firmly grasped the basic presuppositions of Scripture and is thoroughly informed with biblical truth. Only such a mind can think with Christian integrity about the problems of the contemporary world.

Towards the beginning of Romans 12 Paul uses the expression 'the renewing of your mind.' He has just issued his famous appeal to his Roman readers that, in gratitude for God's mercies, they should present their bodies to him as a 'living sacrifice' and as their 'spiritual worship.' Now he goes on to explain how it is possible for God's people to serve him in the world. He sets before us an alternative. One way is to 'be conformed' to this world or 'age,' to its standards (or lack of them), its values (largely materialistic) and its goals (self-centred and godless). These are the characteristics of western culture. Moreover, the prevailing culture (like the prevailing wind) is not easy to stand up against. It is easier to take the line of least resistance and bow down before it, like 'reeds swayed by the wind.' Contemporary secularism is strong and subtle; the pressures to conform are great.

Paul exhorts us, however, not to be conformed to the world, but instead to 'be transformed' by the renewing of our mind with a view to discerning God's pleasing and perfect will. Here, then, is the apostle's assumption both that Christians have or should have a renewed mind, and that our renewed mind will have a radical effect on our lives, since it will enable us to discern and approve God's will, and so transform our behaviour. The sequence is compelling. If we want to live straight, we have to think straight. If we want to think straight, we have to have renewed minds. For once our minds are renewed, we shall become preoccupied not with the way of the world, but with the will of God, which will change us.

Christian conversion means total renewal. The Fall led to total depravity (a doctrine rejected, I suspect, only by those who misunderstand it; it has never meant that every human being is as depraved as he could possibly be, but that every part of our humanness, including our mind, has become distorted by the Fall). So redemption involves total renewal (meaning not that we are now as good as we could be, but that every part of us, including our mind, has been renewed). The contrast is clear. Our old outlook led to conformity to the crowd; our new outlook has led us into moral nonconformity, out of concern for the will of God. Our fallen mind followed the way of the world; our renewed mind is engrossed with the will of God, as revealed in the Word of God. Between the two lies repentance, *metanoia*, a complete change of mind or outlook.

Paul writes not only of a 'renewed mind' but also of 'the mind of Christ.' He exhorts the Philippians: 'Let this mind be in you, which was also in Christ Jesus' (Philippians 2.5 AV). That is, as we study the teaching and example of Jesus, and consciously put our minds under the yoke of his authority (Matthew 11.29), we begin to think as he thought. His mind is gradually formed within us by the Holy Spirit, who is the Spirit of Christ. We see things his way, from his perspective. Our outlook becomes aligned to his. We almost dare to say what the apostle could say: 'we have the mind of Christ' (1 Corinthians 2.16).

'The renewed mind.' 'The mind of Christ.' 'The Christian mind.' Harry Blamires popularised this third expression in his book of that title, which since its publication in 1963 has had widespread influence. By a 'Christian mind' he is referring not to a mind occupied with specifically 'religious' topics, but to a mind which can think about even the most 'secular' topics 'Christianly,' that is, from a Christian perspective. It is not the mind of a schizoid Christian who 'hops in and out of his Christian mentality as the topic of conversation changes from the Bible to the day's newspaper.'[6] No, the Christian mind, he writes, is 'a mind trained, informed, equipped to handle data of secular controversy within a framework of reference which is constructed of Christian presuppositions.'[7]

Mr. Blamires laments the contemporary loss of Christian thinking even among church leaders: 'The Christian mind has succumbed to the secular drift with a degree of weakness and nervelessness unmatched in Christian history.'[8] Having deplored its loss, Harry Blamires sets about canvassing its recovery. He wants to witness the rise of the kind of Christian thinker who 'challenges current prejudices . . . , disturbs the complacent . . . , obstructs the busy pragmatists . . . , questions the very foundations of all about him, and . . . is a nuisance.'[9]

Mr. Blamires then goes on to list what he sees as the six essential 'marks' of a Christian mind: (1) 'its supernatural orientation' (it looks beyond time to eternity, beyond earth to heaven and hell, and meanwhile inhabits a world fashioned, sustained, and 'worried over' by God); (2) 'its awareness of evil' (original sin perverting even the noblest things into instruments of 'hungry vanity'); (3) 'its conception of truth' (the givenness of divine revelation which cannot be compromised); (4) 'its acceptance of authority' (what God has revealed requires from us 'not an egalitarian attachment, but a bending submission'); (5) 'its concern for the person' (a recognition of the value of human personality over against servitude to the machine); and (6) 'its sacramental cast' (for example, recognising sexual love as 'one of God's most efficient instruments' to open man's heart to Reality).

Although these six characteristics of the Christian mind are without doubt some of the most important truths of the biblical revelation, I confess that I have found it hard to commit them to memory, since they appear to be somewhat random and not to cohere into a logically-developed or integrated scheme.

I find it easier, therefore, to adopt the Bible's own framework. For the truly Christian mind has repented of 'proof-texting' (the notion that we can settle every doctrinal and ethical issue by quoting a single, isolated text, whereas God has given us a comprehensive revelation), and instead saturates itself in the whole of Scripture. In particular, it has absorbed the fourfold scheme of biblical history. For the Bible divides human history into epochs, which are marked not by the rise and fall of empires, dynasties or civilisations, but by four major events—the Creation, the Fall, the Redemption, and the Consummation.

First, *the Creation.* It is absolutely foundational to the Christian faith (and therefore to the Christian mind) that in the beginning, when time began, God made the universe out of nothing. He went on to make the planet earth, its land and seas and all their creatures. Finally, as the climax of his creative activity, he made man, male and female, in his own image. The Godlikeness of mankind emerges as the story unfolds: men and women are rational and moral beings (able to understand and respond to God's commands), responsible beings (exercising dominion over nature), social beings (with a capacity to love and to be loved), and spiritual beings (finding their highest fulfilment in knowing and worshipping their Creator). Indeed, the Creator and his human creatures are depicted as walking and talking together in the garden. All this was the Godlikeness which gave Adam and Eve their unique worth and dignity.

Next, *the Fall*. They listened to Satan's lies, instead of to God's truth. In consequence of their disobedience they were driven out of the garden. No greater tragedy has befallen human beings than this, that though made by God like God and for God, they now live without God. All our human alienation, disorientation, and sense of meaninglessness stem ultimately from this. In addition, our relationships with each other have become skewed. Sexual equality was upset: 'Your husband . . . will rule over you' (Genesis 3.16). Pain came to haunt the threshold of motherhood. Cain's jealous hatred of his brother erupted into murder. Even nature was put out of joint. The ground was cursed because of man, the cultivation of the soil became an uphill struggle, and creative work degenerated into drudgery. Over the centuries men and women have slipped from the responsible stewardship of the environment entrusted to them, and have cut down the forests, created deserts and dustbowls, polluted the rivers and seas, and fouled the atmosphere with poisons. 'Original sin' means that our inherited human nature is now twisted with a disastrous self-centredness. Evil is an ingrained, pervasive reality. Although our Godlikeness has not been destroyed, we are yet hostile to God and under his just condemnation.

Thirdly, *the Redemption*. Instead of abandoning or destroying his rebellious creatures, as they deserved, God planned to redeem them. No sooner had man sinned than God promised that the woman's seed would crush the serpent's head (Genesis 3.15), which we recognise as the first prediction of the coming Saviour. God's redemptive purpose began to take shape when he called Abraham and entered into a solemn covenant with him, promising to bless both him and through his posterity all the families of the earth—another promise which we know has been fulfilled in Christ and his worldwide community. God renewed his covenant, this time with Israel, at Mount Sinai, and kept promising through the prophets that there was more, much more, to come in the days of the Messianic Kingdom. Then in the fulness of the time the Messiah came. With him the new age dawned, the Kingdom of God broke in, the end began. Now today, through the death, resurrection, and Spirit-gift of Jesus, God is fulfilling his promise of redemption and remaking marred mankind, not only as individuals, but incorporating them into his new, reconciled community.

Fourth will come *the Consummation*. For one day, when the good news of the Kingdom has been proclaimed throughout the whole world (Matthew 24.14), Jesus Christ will appear in great magnificence. He will raise the dead, judge the world, regenerate the universe, and bring God's Kingdom to its perfection. From it all pain, decay, sin, sorrow, and death will be banished, and in it God will be glorified for ever. Meanwhile, we are living in between times, between Kingdom Come and Kingdom Consummated, between the 'now' and the 'then' of redemption, between the 'already' and the 'not yet.'

Here, then, are four events which correspond to four realities—first the Creation ('the good'), secondly the Fall ('the evil'), thirdly the Redemption ('the new'), and fourthly the Consummation ('the perfect'). This fourfold biblical reality enables Christians to survey the historical landscape within its proper horizons. It supplies the true perspective from which to view the unfolding process between two eternities, the vision of God working out his purpose. It gives us a framework in which to fit everything, a way of integrating our understanding, the possibility of thinking straight, even about the most complex issues.

For the four events or epochs we have been thinking about, especially when grasped in relation to one another, teach major truths about God, man, and society which give direction to our Christian thinking.

The Reality of God

First, the reality of God. The fourfold biblical scheme is essentially God-centred, or at least its four realities are disclosed from

his point of view. Even the Fall, though an act of human disobedience, is presented in the context of divine commandments,
sanctions, and judgment. Thus, it is God who creates, judges, redeems, and perfects. The initiative is his from beginning to end.
That is why the popular cult of meaninglessness is so deeply
offensive to Christians. There is indeed a cluster of popular
attitudes which are fundamentally incompatible with Christian
faith: e.g. the concept of blind evolutionary development, the assertion of human autonomy in art, science, and education, the
declarations that history is random and life is absurd. The Christian mind comes into direct collision with these secular notions.
It insists that human beings can be defined only in relation to
God, that man without God has ceased to be truly man. For we
are creatures who depend on our Creator, sinners who are accountable to him and under his judgment, waifs who are lost
apart from his redemption.

This God-centredness is basic to the Christian mind. The
Christian mind is a godly mind. More than that, it understands
'goodness' above all in terms of 'godliness.' It cannot describe as
'good' a person who is 'ungodly.'

This is the clear testimony of the Bible's Wisdom Literature.
The five books of Wisdom (Job, Psalms, Proverbs, Ecclesiastes,
and the Song of Songs) all focus, in different ways and with different emphases, on what it means to be human and on how suffering, evil, oppression, and love fit into our humanness. The
Book of Ecclesiastes is best known for its pessimistic refrain
'vanity of vanities, all is vanity,' well translated in the New International Version as 'meaningless, meaningless, utterly meaningless.' It demonstrates the folly and futility of a human life
circumscribed by time and space. If life is restricted to the aver-
age brief life span, is overshadowed by pain and injustice, and
culminates for everybody in the same fate, death; if it is also restricted by the dimensions of space to human experiences 'under
the sun,' with no ultimate reference point—then indeed life is as
profitless as 'a chasing after wind.' Only God, Creator and Judge,
Beginning and End, by adding to human life the dimensions of

transcendence and eternity can give it meaning, and so turn folly into wisdom.

Over against the pessimism of Ecclesiastes we set the oft-repeated maxim of the Wisdom Literature, namely 'the fear of the Lord—that is wisdom [or its "beginning" or "principle"], and to shun evil is understanding' (Job 28.28. Cf. Psalms 111.10; Proverbs 1.7, 9.10; Ecclesiastes 12.13). Here are the two major realities of human experience, God and evil. They are not equal realities, for Christians are not dualists. But they dominate life on earth. The one (God) brings human fulfilment, even ecstasy; the other (evil) human alienation, even despair. And wisdom consists in adopting a right attitude to both, loving God and hating evil, 'fearing' God with the worship which acknowledges his infinite worth, and 'shunning' evil in the holiness which despises it for its worthlessness. It is because God has made us spiritual and moral beings that religion and ethics, godliness and goodness, are fundamental to authentic humanness. Hence the tragedy of 'secularism,' the closed world view which denies God and even glories in the spiritual vacuum it creates. T. S. Eliot was right to call it a 'waste land,' and Theodore Roszak in *Where the Wasteland Ends* to characterise it as a desert of the spirit. 'For what science can measure is only a portion of what man can know. Our knowing reaches out to embrace the sacred.' Without transcendence 'the person shrinks.'[10] Secularism not only dethrones God; it destroys human beings.

If, because of the reality of God, the Christian mind is a godly mind, it is also a humble mind. This is another consistent theme of Scripture. When Nebuchadnezzar strutted round the flat roof-top of his palace like a peacock, claiming for himself instead of God the kingdom, the power, and the glory, he went mad. Only when he acknowledged the rule of God and worshipped him were his reason and his kingdom restored to him. Daniel pointed the moral: 'those who walk in pride he is able to humble' (Daniel 4.28–37). It is a sobering story. If pride and madness go together, so do humility and sanity.

Jesus' contemporaries must have been dumbfounded when he

told adults that they had to become like children if they wanted to enter God's Kingdom, and (even worse) that greatness in the Kingdom would be measured by childlike humility. We are too familiar with this teaching; it has lost its power to shock or stun. Yet Jesus not only taught it; he exhibited it. He emptied himself and humbled himself. So now, Paul adds, 'let this mind be in you which was in him.' The medieval moralists were right to see pride as the worst of the 'seven deadly sins' and as the root of the others. There is nothing so obscene as pride, nothing so attractive as humility.

Probably at no point does the Christian mind clash more violently with the secular mind than in its insistence on humility and its implacable hostility to pride. The wisdom of the world despises humility. Western culture has imbibed more than it knows of the power philosophy of Nietzsche. The world's model, like Nietzsche's, is the 'superman'; the model of Jesus remains the little child.

Thus the Reality of God (as Creator, Lord, Redeemer, Father, Judge) gives to the Christian mind its first and most fundamental characteristic. Christians refuse to honour anything which dishonours God. We learn to evaluate everything in terms of the glory it gives to, or withholds from, God. That is why, to the Christian mind, wisdom is the fear of God and the preeminent virtue is humility.

The Paradox of Man

I turn now from God to man, from the unalloyed splendour which characterises whatever is 'divine' to the painful ambiguity which attaches to everything 'human.'

We have already seen that the biblical understanding of mankind takes equal account of the Creation and the Fall. This constitutes 'the paradox of man.' We human beings have both a unique dignity as creatures made in God's image and a unique depravity as sinners under his judgment. The former gives us hope; the latter places a limit on our expectations. Our Christian critique of the secular mind is that it tends to be either too naively optimistic or too negatively pessimistic in its estimates of the human condition, whereas the Christian mind, firmly rooted in biblical realism, both celebrates the glory and deplores the shame of our human being. We can behave like God in whose image we were made, only to descend to the level of the beasts. We are able to think, choose, create, love, and worship, but also to refuse to think, to choose evil, to destroy, to hate, and to worship ourselves. We build churches and drop bombs. We develop intensive care units for the critically ill and use the same technology to torture political enemies who presume to disagree with us. This is 'man,' a strange bewildering paradox, dust of earth and breath of God, shame and glory. So, as the Christian mind applies itself to the life of man on earth, his personal, social, and political affairs, it seeks to remember what a paradoxical creature he is—noble and ignoble, rational and irrational, loving and selfish.

Perhaps I can best illustrate this dialectic by taking two examples, first our sexuality and secondly the political process.

It is pertinent to begin with our sexuality, partly because we are all of us sexual beings, and partly because, of all the social revolutions taking place this century, the sexual revolution may well be the profoundest. Sexual roles (masculinity and femininity), the context for sexual intercourse (in or out of marriage), whether the traditional understandings of marriage and the family can (or even should) survive, the option of homosexual partnerships, contraception, *in vitro* fertilisation, AID (Artificial Insemination by Donor), easy abortion and easy divorce—these are some aspects of human sexuality about which radical questions are being asked today. Although the Bible gives clear instructions on some of them, we will be far better placed to grapple with individual issues if we first gain a bird's-eye view of sexuality in general by seeing it in the light of Scripture's fourfold scheme.

According to Genesis 1 and 2, God created man male and female in his image from the beginning and told them to be fruitful. Although he pronounced creation 'good,' he needed to add that 'it is not good for the man to be alone.' And he went on to ordain that the sexual companionship of man and woman was to be consummated in the mysteries of the 'one flesh' experience. Thus human sexuality, marriage, sexual intercourse, and the family are all part of the creative purpose of God. Marriage (as a publicly pledged, permanent, exclusive, heterosexual union) is not a human but a divine institution, which therefore in itself is not affected by changing culture. Sexual intimacy within marriage is a good gift of a good Creator.

But after the Creation came the Fall. Sin has distorted our sexuality, as it has every other human instinct, faculty, and appetite. Sex has surely become a far more imperious drive than God originally intended. Unnatural sexual deviations have arisen. Although sexual love can still be enjoyed, and even wonderingly celebrated as in the Song of Songs, nevertheless it is also often spoiled by selfish demands, fears, exploitation, and cruelty.

The redeeming work of Christ through his Spirit has made possible a whole new attitude to sex. This includes (in addition to a recognition of the Creator's purpose and gift) the control and sanctification of our sexual drive, a vision of self-giving love in marriage as a reflection of the relation between Christ and his church, and a partnership between the sexes which, while not denying the responsible and caring headship which God has given to man (rooted in creation not culture), also rejoices that in their relationship to God 'there is neither . . . male nor female,' since they are now equally justified in Christ and equally adopted into God's family (Galatians 3.26–29).

What about the End? In the next world after the resurrection, Jesus said, 'they will neither marry nor be given in marriage; they will be like the angels in heaven' (Mark 12.25). So, although love is eternal, marriage is not. Procreation will no longer be necessary. Relationships of love will transcend the physical, and will probably be less exclusive (though surely no less rich) than in marriage. The importance of adding this fourth stage should be clear. It contains a message both for the married (lest the union become selfish to the point even of idolatry) and for the single (that marriage is not indispensable to the attainment of full humanness).

As we try to respond Christianly to the radical sexual challenges of today, we shall find it easier to struggle with particular issues within this general biblical framework.

My second example related to 'the paradox of man' concerns the political process. The nature of man is arguably the basic political issue of the twentieth century. It is certainly one of the chief points of conflict between Marx and Jesus, and therefore between the East and the West, namely whether human beings have any absolute value because of which they must be respected, or whether their value is only relative to the community because of which they may be exploited. More simply, are the people the servants of the institution, or is the institution the servant of the people? As John S. Whale has written, 'ideologies . . . are really anthropologies'[11]; they reflect different doctrines of man.

Christians should be careful not to 'baptise' any political ideology (whether of the right, the left or the centre) as if it contained a monopoly of truth and goodness. At best a political ideology and its programme are only an approximation to Christian or biblical ideas. The fact is that, at least in some parts of the world, Christians are to be found in virtually every political party and are able to defend their membership on conscientious Christian grounds. Thus, to indulge in a blunt oversimplification, both main political ideologies in western societies appeal to Christians for different reasons. Capitalism appeals because it encourages individual human initiative and enterprise, but also repels because it seems not to care that the weak succumb to the fierce competition it engenders. Socialism appeals, on the other hand, because it has great compassion for the poor and the weak, but also repels because it seems not to care that individual initiative and enterprise are smothered by the very big government which it engenders.

Each attracts because it emphasises a truth about man, either the need to give free play to his creative abilities or the need to protect him from injustice. Each repels because it fails to take with equal seriousness the complementary truth. Both can be liberating. But both can also be oppressive, as we see in the extreme totalitarian régimes of both left and right. A wit has put this well: 'The difference between Capitalism and Socialism is that in Capitalism man exploits man, while in Socialism it is the other way round!' It is understandable that many Christians dream of a third alternative which overcomes the present confrontation and incorporates the best features of both.

Whatever our political colour may be, all Christians tend to advocate democracy (popularly defined as 'government of the people by the people'). Not that it is 'perfect or all-wise,' as Winston Churchill conceded in the House of Commons on 11 November 1947.

'Indeed,' he continued, 'it has been said that democracy is the worst form of government—except for all those other forms that have been tried from time to time.' The fact is that it is the wisest and safest form of government yet devised. This is because it reflects the paradox of man. On the one hand, it takes the Creation seriously (that is, human dignity), because it refuses to govern human beings without their consent, and insists instead on giving them a responsible share in the decision-making process. On the other hand, it takes the Fall seriously (that is, human depravity), because it refuses to concentrate power in the hands of one person or of a few people, and insists instead on dispersing it, thus protecting human beings from their own pride and folly. Reinhold Niebuhr put it succinctly: 'man's capacity for justice makes democracy possible; but man's inclination to injustice makes democracy necessary.'[12]

The Future of Society

The third sphere to which it may be helpful to apply the Bible's fourfold scheme concerns the possibility of social change. What expectation should we have that society can improve? On this issue Christians of different traditions are to be found along a broad spectrum.

'Liberal' Christians have tended to be social activists. Because of their almost boundless confidence in man, they dream dreams of building Utopia (sometimes mistakenly identified as 'the Kingdom of God') on earth.

'Evangelical' Christians, on the other hand, have tended—at least earlier this century—to be social quietists. Because of their gloomy view of human depravity, they lack all confidence in man (at least until he has been born again). They therefore consider social action a waste of time and social transformation all but impossible.

I have deliberately expressed both positions in their more extreme form. Stated thus, the polarisation fails to hold together the two parts of the human paradox.

Because human beings are made in the image of God, and the divine image (though marred) has not been wholly lost, they retain some perception of the just and compassionate society which would please him, and some desire to bring it about. On the whole, all humankind still prefers peace to war, justice to oppression, harmony to discord, order to chaos. So social change is possible, and indeed has happened. In many parts of the world we can see rising standards of hygiene and health care, a greater respect for women and children, the increasing availability of education, a clearer recognition of human rights, a growing concern to conserve the natural environment, and better conditions in mine, factory, and prison. Much of this has been due (directly or indirectly) to Christian influence, although by no means all social reformers have been committed Christians. But whenever God's people have been effective as salt and light in the community, there has been less social decay and more social uplift. In the United States, for example, especially after the early nineteenth-century awakening associated with Charles G. Finney, 'born-again Christians were in the forefront of every major social reform in America during the 1830s. They spearheaded the abolitionist movement, the temperance movement, the peace movement, and the early feminist movement.'[13]

Because human beings are fallen, however, and inherit a twist of self-centredness, we shall never succeed in building a perfect society. Improvement—yes; perfect justice—no. Utopian dreams are unrealistic; they belong to the world of fantasy. All human plans, though launched with great hopes, have to some degree disappointed the planners, for they have foundered on the rock of human selfishness. Christians have usually remembered this. As William Temple put it, 'its assertion of Original Sin should make the Church intensely realistic and conspicuously free from Utopianism.'[14]

Certainly the evangelical Christians who gathered in Lausanne at the great International Congress on World Evangelisation declared forthrightly in their Covenant: 'We . . . reject as a proud, self-confident dream the notion that man can ever build a utopia on earth.'[15] It is socialists who have tended to be too optimistic about human achievement. Professor C. E. M. Joad was a good example. Brought up on the Church of England's 1662 Book of Common Prayer, its confessions and collects, he began by believing in the inherent sinfulness of human beings. But later he discarded this notion in favour of man's 'infinite perfectibility,' until World War II shattered this illusion and convinced him again that 'evil is endemic in man.' He wrote candidly in his book *Recovery of Belief* (1952): 'It is because we rejected the doctrine of original sin that we on the Left were always being disappointed; disappointed by the refusal of people to be reasonable, by the subservience of intellect to emotion, by the failure of true Socialism to arrive . . . , above all, by the recurrent fact of war.'[16]

It is difficult to avoid extremes of pessimism and optimism about the possibility of social change. Robert McNamara nearly did, in what has been described as perhaps his 'most eloquent speech' while in office as U.S. Defence Secretary: 'All the evidence of history suggests that man is indeed a rational animal, but with a nearly infinite capacity for folly. His history seems largely a halting but persistent effort to raise his reason above his animality. He draws blueprints for Utopia, but never quite gets it built.'[17] But even this sounds a trifle cynical.

How then can we sum up an attitude to the possibility of social change which reflects 'neither the easy optimism of the humanist, nor the dark pessimism of the cynic, but the radical realism of the Bible'?[18] How can we do equal justice to the truths of creation, fall, redemption, and consummation? I suggest that the biblical balance is well expressed by Paul in 1 Thessalonians 1.9, 10, where he describes the results of conversion from idols to God as being 'to serve the living and true God, and to wait for his Son from heaven.' The combination of 'serving' and 'waiting' is striking, since the former is actively getting busy for Christ on earth, while the latter is passively looking for him to come from heaven. We must serve, but there are limits to what we can achieve. We must wait, but have no liberty to do so in idleness. Thus 'working' and 'waiting' go together. The need to wait for Christ from heaven will rescue us from the presumption which thinks we can do everything; the need to work for Christ on earth will rescue us from the pessimism which thinks we can do nothing. Only a Christian mind which has developed a biblical perspective can enable us to preserve this balance.

I began this chapter by admitting the complexity of the problems of personal and social ethics which confront us today. Neat, cut-and-dried solutions are usually impossible. Simplistic short-cuts, which ignore the real issues, are unhelpful. At the same time, it is not Christian to give up in despair.

We need to remember for our encouragement that God has given us four gifts.

His first gift is a mind with which to think. He has made us rational, intelligent creatures. He still forbids us to behave like horses and mules which lack understanding, and tells us in our thinking to be not babies but adults.[19]

Secondly, he has given us the Bible and its witness to Christ, in order to direct and control our thinking. As we absorb its teaching, our thoughts will increasingly conform to his. This is not because we memorise a lot of proof texts, which we trot out at appropriate moments, each text labelled to answer its own question. It is rather that we have grasped the great themes and principles of Scripture and the fourfold framework we have been considering.

God's third gift is the Holy Spirit, the Spirit of truth, to open up the Scriptures to us and illumine our minds to understand and apply them.

Fourthly, God has given us the Christian community as the context in which to do our thinking. Its heterogeneity is the best safeguard against blinkered vision. For the church has members of both sexes, and of all ages, temperaments, experiences, and cultures. With rich insights contributed to the interpretation of Scripture from such a diversity of backgrounds, it will be hard to maintain our prejudices.

With these four gifts, especially in relation to each other—a mind, a textbook, a Teacher, and a School—it should be possible for us to develop an increasingly Christian mind and to learn to think straight.

Chapter Three

Pluralism: Should We Impose Our Views?

WE ACCEPT THAT WE SHOULD GET INVOLVED. AND WE STRUGGLE TO think Christianly about the issues. In consequence, we develop some quite strong convictions. But others do not share them. Indeed, Christians find themselves increasingly out of step with the post-Christian society of which they are a part. So how can we hope to influence our country into becoming more Christian again, in its laws, its institutions, and its culture? Should Christians attempt to impose their views on a largely non-Christian nation?

In Europe and America, and in those Commonwealth countries which inherited the 'Christian civilisation' of the west, we certainly have to come to terms with the new pluralism. John Briggs has given us a competent historical survey of this development in his essay 'From Christendom to Pluralism.'[1] Pluralism is largely due to two factors. The first is the process of secularisation, seen as the diminishing influence of the church in both people and institutions. Accurate statistics are notoriously hard to obtain and to interpret. It seems to be clear, however, that membership of the Protestant churches of England, Wales, and Scotland dropped from 13 percent of the population in 1920 to 8 percent in 1970, which represents a loss of almost 40 percent of members in 50 years. Again, during the 11-year period from 1971 to 1981, 828 Church of England churches were declared redundant, and were either scheduled for demolition or appropriated to other uses (cultural, residential, etc.). It is true that the tide may have begun to turn. According to the most recent opinion poll undertaken by the research department of the Bible Society, and published in 1983, 15 percent of the English population claim to attend church once a week or more.[2] Nevertheless, in contrast to half a century ago, let alone the nineteenth century, there can be no doubt that the church has lost a great deal of ground.

Alongside the Christian decline has gone an increase in non-Christian alternatives, for the second cause of pluralism is the liberal immigration policy of the immediate post-war years. As a result, most western countries now include in their population sizeable ethnic groups from Africa, Asia, the Middle East, and the Caribbean. This makes possible for all of us a rich experience of cultural diversity. But it also leads to religious competition and to consequent demands for recognition in the country's educational system, laws, and institutions. In 1980 the adult membership of non-Christian religious groups in the United Kingdom was as follows:[3]

Muslims	600,000
Sikhs	150,000
Jews	110,915
Hindus	120,000
Mormons	91,032
Jehovah's Witnesses	85,321

If we add together the total adult UK membership of all non-Christian religious minorities (including spiritualists, Christian Scientists, Christadelphians, and others), it comes to nearly one and a half millions, almost twice the combined total UK adult membership of the Methodist and Baptist churches. As for unbelievers, since the most generous estimate of the size of all religious communities in Britain (including children and nonpractising adherents) is 73 percent, there must be 27 percent who make no religious profession at all.

Elsewhere in the world, even if Christians represent a substantial minority, the predominant culture is either Hindu or Buddhist, Jewish or Islamic, Marxist or secular. So here too, usually in a more acute form, Christians are faced with the same dilemma. In many issues they believe they know the will of God. They also believe it is their Christian duty to pray and work for God's will to be done. Should they hope to impose their Christian convictions on non-Christians? If it is possible, is it desirable? Even if they could, should they try?

The two commonest responses to these questions represent opposite extremes. One is 'imposition,' the crusading attempt to coerce people by legislation to accept the Christian way. The other is 'laissez-faire,' the defeatist decision to leave people alone in their non-Christian ways, and not interfere or try to influence them in any way. We need to look carefully at these alternatives, with some historical examples, before we shall be ready for a third and better option.

Imposition

Here are Christians with a commendable zeal for God. They believe in revelation, and they care deeply about God's revealed truth and will. They long to see society reflecting it. So the desire to achieve this end by force is an understandable temptation.

My first historical illustration is the Inquisition in Europe, which was a special tribunal set up by the Roman Catholic Church in the thirteenth century to combat heresy. Suspected heretics were first hunted out, then invited to confess, and then if they refused brought to trial. By Pope Innocent IV's bull *Ad Extirpanda* in 1252, torture was permitted in addition to trial. Impenitent heretics were punished by excommunication, imprisonment or confiscation of goods, or were handed over to the State to be burned alive. The Inquisition lasted about three hundred years. It was suppressed in 1542, although the Spanish Inquisition (which was the most cruel), instituted at the end of the fifteenth century by Ferdinand and Isabella for purposes of national security, especially against Jews, Moors, and Protestants, was abolished only in the year 1834. Today, I imagine, Christians of all traditions are deeply ashamed that such methods could ever have been used in the name of Jesus Christ. The Inquisition is a horrible blot on the pages of church history, never to be reinstated. Yet dictatorships of the extreme left and right are still guilty of trying by force to abolish opposition and compel assent. All Christians affirm, however, that totalitarianism and torture are both wholly incompatible with the mind and Spirit of Jesus.

My second and more recent historical example is 'Prohibition' in the United States, namely the legal ban on the manufacture and sale of alcoholic liquor. The National Prohibition Party was formed in 1869 by a group of white Protestants. Their motives were admirable. Dismayed by the increase of heavy drinking and drunkenness, especially among poor immigrants and perceiving this as a threat to public order, they committed themselves to work for the total prohibition of alcoholic beverages. In 1895 the Anti-Saloon League of America was founded by a group of church leaders, and after a campaign of about twenty-five years Congress passed in 1919 the Eighteenth Amendment to the Constitution, prohibiting the manufacture, sale, and transportation of liquor. It came into force a year later, and forty-six out of forty-eight states had ratified it within about two years.

The result, however, was that the law was widely broken. 'Bootleggers' made, sold, and smuggled alcoholic drinks illegally, and 'speakeasies' (stores in which liquor was sold clandestinely) flourished. So in 1933, fourteen years after the so-called 'Noble Experiment' began, President Roosevelt signed the Twenty-first Amendment, voiding the Eighteenth and ending Prohibition. Far from abolishing alcohol-abuse, it had provoked and increased it. And the law had been brought into disrepute.

So was Prohibition foisted on the country, or did the people want it? Opinions differ. The 'drys' claim that there was a national consensus; the 'wets' that this was obtained only by legislative action, not direct popular vote, and only when the nation's mind was preoccupied with America's entry into World War I. John Kobler writes: 'The accessible evidence confirms neither claim. It precludes any flat answer and leaves the question for ever unsettled.' Nevertheless, this is how he concludes his historical enquiry: 'In sum, it appeared that rural, agricultural America with its large Protestant, native-born population thrust prohibition upon urban, industrial America, with its heterogeneity of races, religions, and foreign backgrounds.'[4]

Looking back at these two examples, one European and the other American, the Inquisition was an attempt to impose belief, and Prohibition an attempt to impose behaviour. Both were seen in the end to be unproductive, for you cannot force people to believe what they do not believe, or practise what they do not want to practise. Similarly, to imagine today that we can force Christian convictions and standards on Europe and America is totally unrealistic. It is a foolish nostalgia for a Christendom which has long since vanished.

Laissez-faire

The opposite to 'imposition,' I suggest, is 'laissez-faire.' The term was originally used in the eighteenth century of Free Trade economists, and the concept dominated nineteenth-century society. It had no overtones of the lackadaisical about it. On the contrary, it was a principled belief in the necessity of non-interference by government. The use of the word has changed with the centuries, however, and in popular parlance today it describes a mood of apathy and indifference. It is applied to citizens as much as to governments. Far from imposing our views, we say, we will not even propagate or commend them. We shall leave other people alone to mind their own business, as we devoutly hope they will leave us alone to mind ours. Laissez-faire has even sometimes been an attitude adopted by Christian people in the name of tolerance. Tolerant in spirit Christians should

certainly be, showing respect towards those who think and behave differently. Socially tolerant too, in the sense that we should
want to see political and religious minorities accepted in the
community and protected by law, just as the Christian minority
in a non-Christian country expects to be legally free to profess,
practise, and propagate the gospel. But how can Christians be intellectually tolerant of opinions we know to be false or actions
we know to be evil? What kind of unprincipled indulgence is
this? Societies smell sweet or acrid in the nostrils of God. He is
not indifferent to questions of social justice, so how can his people be? To remain silent and inactive when error or evil is being
perpetrated has very serious consequences. For the Christian option has then gone by default. Is it not at least partly because
Christians have failed to raise their voices for Jesus Christ, that
whole nations have slipped their Christian moorings and drifted
away from them?

The gravest modern example of Christian laissez-faire is the
failure of German churches to speak out against the Nazis' treatment of the Jews. It is a long and dismal story, thoroughly documented by Richard Gutteridge in his book *Open Thy Mouth for the
Dumb*.[5] He traces Christian complicity in German antisemitism
back to the nineteenth century, when Christianity became identified with a mystical German patriotism, which increased after
defeat in World War I. It was at this time that several misguided
attempts were made to theologise the intrinsic value of the Aryan
'Volk.' For example, Paul Althaus wrote in 1932: 'It is God's will
that we maintain our Race and our Volkstum in purity, that we
remain German men, and do not become a bastard-Volk of Jewish Aryan blood.'[6] At that time the church seemed to be in alli-
ance with the National Socialist Movement. Only a few brave
voices (like those of Karl Barth and Paul Tillich) were raised in
protest. But meanwhile the 'Faith Movement of German Christians,' under the patronage of the Nazi Party, affirmed the Aryan
Race.

After Hitler came to power in 1933 a law was passed to purge
the Civil Service of officials of non-Aryan descent, and, incredi-

ble as it may seem, the racially compromised 'German Christians' wanted to apply this 'Aryan Clause' to the church. Several synods adopted it, against the opposition of men like Martin Niemöller, Walter Künneth, Hans Lilje, and Dietrich Bonhoeffer. Yet 'the Evangelical Church never spoke out officially against the Aryan legislation in general.' Bonhoeffer was deeply upset by the church's silence and frequently quoted Proverbs 31.8, 'Open thy mouth for the dumb. . . .'[7]

In the terrible pogrom of November 1938, 119 synagogues were set on fire (of which 76 were destroyed), 20,000 Jews were arrested, shops were looted, and prominent Jewish citizens publicly humiliated. The general public was aghast, and some church leaders protested. But 'there was no chance of the Evangelical Church as a whole voicing her horror and indignation, and the Catholic Church kept almost completely silent, and their hierarchy found no word to say.'[8]

Hitler's appalling 'Final Solution,' which he had already decided upon before World War II broke out, began to be implemented in 1941. Not until two years later, however, did a conference of Lutheran Church leaders resolve to attack the Reich government for its anti-Jewish atrocities. This is how Richard Gutteridge sums up his thesis: 'The Church as Church did not find a decisive word from Scripture as a whole to embrace the issue as a whole. . . . Throughout the Conflict nobody in a position of authority made a full and plain denunciation of anti-semitism as such.'[9] Barth called it 'the sin against the Holy Ghost' and a 'rejection of the grace of God.'[10] Some other church officials were equally bold, and paid dearly for their courage. But when Evangelical Church leaders met soon after the end of the war, and issued their 'Stuttgart Declaration,' they had to acknowledge: 'it is our self-indictment that we have not made a more courageous confession.'[11]

Gutteridge concludes: 'The ultimate failure of the Church lay not in the inability of bishops and synods to make plain and outspoken pronouncements in public,' though it included that, but rather 'what was missing was a spontaneous outburst at any point by ordinary decent Christian folk. . . . A really widespread, public, visible expression of righteous indignation would have had to have been taken very seriously indeed by the Nazi leaders, and would assuredly have had a profound effect in curbing the most iniquitous excesses and brutalities, if not in bringing about the downfall of so monstrous and unprincipled a tyranny.'[12]

The story Richard Gutteridge tells speaks for itself. It needs no additional comment from me. The complicity of the 'German Christians,' who failed to develop a biblical critique of the Nazis' blatant racism, should be enough to outlaw laissez-faire for ever. Could they not have prevented the Holocaust?

Persuasion

Better than the extremes of 'imposition' and 'laissez-faire' is the strategy of 'persuasion' by argument. This is the way the Christian mind advocates, for it arises naturally from the biblical doctrines of God and man.

The living God of the biblical revelation, who created and sustains the universe, intended the human beings he made to live in loving community. Moreover his righteousness is an essential expression of his love. He loves justice and hates oppression. He champions the cause of the poor, the alien, the widow, and the orphan. He feeds the hungry, clothes the naked, heals the sick, finds the lost. He wants all mankind to be saved and to come to know the truth in his Son Jesus Christ. Now this biblical vision of God profoundly affects our attitude to society, since God's concerns inevitably become his people's too. We also will respect men and women made in God's image, seek justice, hate injustice, care for the needy, guard the dignity of work, recognise the necessity of rest, maintain the sanctity of marriage, be zealous for the honour of Jesus Christ, and long that every knee will do homage to him and every tongue confess him. Why? Because all these are God's concerns. How can we acquiesce in things which passionately displease him, or affect nonchalance about things he is strongly committed to? The policy of laissez-faire is inconceivable to Christians who hold a biblical doctrine of God.

But then the policy of imposition is equally impossible to those who hold a biblical doctrine of man, for God made man male and female to be responsible beings. He told them to be fruitful (exercise their powers of procreation), to subdue the earth and rule its creatures, to work and to rest, and to obey him ('you may . . . you must not . . .'). These injunctions would be meaningless if God had not endowed man with two unique gifts—conscience (to discern between alternatives) and freedom (to choose between them). The rest of the Bible confirms this. It is assumed throughout that human beings are moral beings, who are accountable for their actions. They know the moral law, since it is 'written on their hearts,' and are exhorted to obedience and warned of the penalties of disobedience. But they are never coerced. No compulsion is ever used. Only persuasion by argument: 'Come now, let us reason together, says the Lord' (Isaiah 1.18).

A basic ground for this is that the human conscience must be treated with the greatest respect. Paul expresses his personal determination 'to keep my conscience clear before God and man' (Acts 24.16). He also has much to say about other people's consciences. They may be 'strong' (well educated and free) or 'weak' (over-scrupulous and full of qualms). But whatever the condition of a person's conscience, even when it is mistaken it is to be respected. Weak consciences need to be strengthened, and deceiving consciences enlightened, but there must be no bullying of consciences. Only in the most extreme circumstances should anybody be induced to act against his conscience. In general, consciences are to be educated, not violated.

This principle, which arises out of the Christian doctrine of man, should affect our social behaviour and institutions. It is the reason why Christians oppose autocracy and favour democracy. Autocracy crushes consciences; democracy (at least in theory) respects them, since democratic governments derive 'their just powers from the consent of the governed' (The American Declaration of Independence). Once laws have been promulgated, however, all citizens (in a democracy as in an autocracy) are under constraint to obey them. They may not do as they please.

Yet in matters of great moment (e.g. conscription in time of war) a civilised government will allow 'conscientious objection.' This provision is also the product of a Christian mind.

So the biblical doctrines of both God and man guide our behaviour in a pluralist society, the former ruling out laissez-faire, and the latter imposition. Because God is who he is, we cannot be indifferent when his truth and law are flouted, but because man is who he is, we cannot try to impose them by force.

What, then, should Christians do? We should seek to educate the public conscience to know and desire the will of God. The church should seek to be the conscience of the nation. If we cannot impose God's will by legislation, nor can we convince people of it merely by biblical quotation. For these are examples of 'authority from above,' which people resent and resist. More effective is 'authority from below,' the intrinsic truth and value of a thing which is self-evident and therefore self-authenticating. (Not that the two are incompatible; God's authority is essentially both.) This principle applies equally in evangelism and social action.

In evangelism we should neither try to force people to believe the gospel, nor remain silent as if we were indifferent to their response, nor rely exclusively on the dogmatic proclamation of biblical texts (vital as authoritative biblical exposition is), but rather, like the apostles, reason with people from both nature and Scripture, commending God's gospel to them by rational arguments.

In social action, similarly, we should neither try to impose Christian standards by force on an unwilling public, nor remain silent and inactive before the contemporary landslide, nor rely exclusively on the dogmatic assertion of biblical values, but rather reason with people about the benefits of Christian morality, commending God's law to them by rational arguments. We believe that God's laws are both good in themselves and universal in their application because, far from being arbitrary, they fit the human beings God has made. This was God's claim for his laws from the beginning. He gave them, he said, 'for your own good' (Deuteronomy 10.13), and pleaded with the people to obey them 'so that it might go well with them and their children for ever' (Deuteronomy 5.29). There was thus an essential correspondence between what was 'good and right in the eyes of the Lord' and what was 'well with them' (Deuteronomy 12.28). The 'good' and the 'well' coincided. We believe, moreover, that everybody has an inkling that this is so. But because they may be either unable or unwilling to acknowledge it, we have to deploy arguments to demonstrate that God's laws are for the wellbeing both of individuals and of society.

We therefore need doctrinal apologetic in evangelism (arguing the truth of the gospel) and ethical apologetic in social action (arguing the goodness of the moral law). Apologists of both kinds are wanted urgently in today's church and world.

Examples of Persuasion by Argument

Let me try to supply some examples. I begin with the highly controversial question of *religious and moral education*. In the United States, of course, because of the rigorous separation of church and state, religious teaching is not permitted in the public schools.

In England, however, since education was pioneered by the church, successive Education Acts have required the state schools to provide religious education. The famous 1944 Education Act, steered through Parliament by R. A. Butler, made compulsory both a daily assembly for worship and religious instruction in the classroom, according to an agreed syllabus. During the forty years which have elapsed since then, as the influence of the church has declined, and society has become more pluralist, the forces of secular humanism have mustered. Now the cry is for the comparative study of different religions, ideologies, and moral systems, with no preferential treatment being given to any one. This demand is understandable. We certainly should not compel (say) Jewish or Moslem children to receive Christian instruction (the Butler Act included a conscience clause to this effect), and we should make arrangements for such children, if they and their parents wish, to receive instruction in their own religion (the Butler Act provided for 'withdrawal' classes for this purpose). But what about the whole attitude, atmosphere, and approach of the school? Education is the process of enabling persons to grow into maturity. So we cannot define maturity without defining personhood, and we certainly cannot define personhood without reference to values of belief and behaviour, that is, without reference to religion and morality. What values shall public education teach and commend, then? The smorgasbord approach is irresponsible, since children lack the criteria by which to choose; they need to be helped to evaluate the diversity set before them. And neutrality is impossible. Value-free education is a contradiction in terms. If Christian values are not commended, then secular values will take their place. What, then, is the case for Christian education in pluralist England? We cannot base our argument on the uniqueness and finality of Christ, however strongly we may believe in him. But we could defend a Christian bias in English education on at least three grounds.

(1) The Great Majority of English Residents Are Still at Least Nominally Christian

Although, according to the 1983 poll conducted under Bible Society auspices, only 15 percent of the population attend church once a week or more, 64 percent consider their religious affiliation to be 'Church of England,' and, if the Roman Catholic and Free Churches are added, 84 percent consider themselves to be affiliated to a Christian church. This majority may have to be described as silent, inactive, and uncommitted. But it is a significant indication where their general sympathy lies.

(2) There is the Question of Acceptance

Christianity can claim preferential treatment because it has received a testing, and consequent acceptance, which in combination is longer (historically) and broader (geographically) than any other religion or ideology. Hinduism is older, but is largely restricted to India and to Indians of the dispersion. Marxism can claim to be a worldwide ideology like Christianity, but it is only a century old and has not endured such a rigorous testing.

(3) Christianity is Fundamental to Britain's Cultural Inheritance

Christianity is the cement which binds together Britain's history, laws, institutions, and national way of life. Even immigrants and British-born ethnic minorities, who profess another religion, should nevertheless receive instruction in the origins and culture of the country of their adoption.

I turn, as my second example, from education to *sex ethics*. The Christian standards of chastity before marriage and fidelity within it are increasingly challenged and repudiated. Sexual promiscuity is spreading. Experimental living together before marriage is not only widely practised, but widely recommended. Cohabitation without marriage, not just in the old sense of *de facto* 'common law marriage' but in the sense of deliberately dispensing with marriage altogether as an obsolete custom, now provokes little if any social displeasure. Wife-swopping is regarded as an amusing suburban game. Open 'marriages,' in which the husband knows his wife has other sexual partners, and the wife knows the same about her husband, and both approve of the fact and even encourage it, are not unusual. In some circumstances a series of successive marriages through easy divorce is regarded as 'enriching' (the suffering of the children is ignored or rationalised), and a homosexual partnership is increasingly considered a legitimate alternative to a heterosexual marriage.

In the face of this sexual revolution, Christians should of course both themselves obey, and make known to others, the unchanging standards of God's law. Nevertheless, it will not be enough to climb Mount Sinai and proclaim the Ten Commandments from that pinnacle of authority. Even when people are converted and regenerated (which remains our paramount concern and the surest route to moral uprightness), they still need reasons for obedience. So what arguments can we deploy?

The first is anthropological. It was Raymond Johnston, Director of CARE Trust, who in his 1978 London Lectures in Contemporary Christianity introduced me to J. D. Unwin's book *Sex and Culture* (1934). He describes it as 'one of the monumental works of comparative anthropology.'[13] Unwin confessed that he began his investigation 'with carefree open-mindedness' and 'in all innocence.' With no axe to grind, and no idea where his researches might lead him, he wanted to test the conjecture that civilisation and sexual self-control were related to each other. He studied eighty primitive and sixteen civilised societies, and found that a society's cultural energy (art, science, technology, etc.) increases as its sexual energy is controlled.

His study of certain 'vigorous societies' revealed that 'in each case they reduced their sexual opportunity to a minimum by the adoption of absolute monogamy; in each case the ensuing compulsory continence produced great social energy. The group within the society which suffered the greatest continence displayed the greatest energy, and dominated the society.' Conversely, whenever monogamy was modified, the society's cultural energy decreased. The conclusion of his book was that if a vigorous society 'wishes to display its productive energy for a long time,' it must regulate relations between the sexes by practising monogamy. Then 'its inherited tradition would be continually enriched; it would achieve a higher culture than has yet been attained; by the action of human entropy (sc. the generation of fresh cultural energy) its tradition would be augmented and refined in a manner which surpasses our present understanding.'[14] Freud had taught similarly that the flourishing of culture and the restraining of instincts belong together.

To this sociological evidence a psychological argument may be added. It is well known that male and female sexual experiences differ. The male sexual appetite is largely physical, is quickly aroused and quickly satisfied. With women, however, sexual intercourse is not *in itself* a wholly satisfying experience, for it arouses other desires which are not so easily met—desires for the security of husband, home, and children. For men to arouse such desires, when they have no intention of fulfilling them, can only be described as cruel.[15]

I recently read a confirmation of this in an unlikely place, namely the November 1977 edition of the American magazine *Seventeen*. It carried an article entitled 'The Case Against Living Together,' which took the form of an interview with Dr. Nancy Moore Clatworthy, a sociologist at Ohio State University in Columbus, Ohio. For ten years she had been studying the phenomenon of unmarried couples living together. When she began, she was predisposed towards it. Young people had told her it was 'wonderful,' and she had believed them. It seemed to her a 'sensible' arrangement, 'a useful step in courtship,' during which couples got to know each other. But her research (which involved the testing of hundreds of couples, married and unmarried) led her to change her mind. 'The things people say living together is doing for them, it's not doing,' she said. The problem was specially with the girls, whom she found uptight, fearful, and looking 'past the rhetoric to the possible pain and agony.' She made two points in particular. First, regarding problems. 'In the areas of adjustment, happiness and respect,' couples who had lived together before marriage had *more* problems than those who had married first. They also argued more, e.g. about money, friends, and sex. 'In *every* area the couples who had lived together before marriage disagreed more often than the couples who had not.' It was evident, she concluded, that living together first does not solve problems.

Dr. Clatworthy's second point was about commitment. 'Commitment is the expectation a person has about the outcome of a relationship. . . . Commitment is what makes marriage, living together or any human relationship work.' But 'knowing that something is temporary affects the degree of commitment to it.' So unmarried couples are less than wholehearted in working to sustain and protect their relationship; and consequently 75 percent of them break up. It is specially the girls who are badly hurt. Nancy Clatworthy concludes: 'Statistically, you're much better off marrying than living together. . . . For people who are in love anything less than a full commitment is a cop-out.'

When anthropology, sociology, and psychology all point in the same direction, the argument is powerful. We should not be

afraid to use it. Nor should we be surprised about this conver-
gence, because God has written his law in two places, on stone
tablets and on the tablets of the human heart (Romans 2.14f.).
The moral law is not alien to human beings, therefore. It is 'natural law.' There is a fundamental correspondence between Scripture and nature.

Religious education and sexual morality are only two examples of the need to deploy arguments in our defence and com-
mendation of Christian social ethics. We should seek to develop
the same strategy in every sphere. The 'just war theory,' for instance, is a line of reasoning which is not expressly Christian. Although it has been developed by great Christian thinkers like
Augustine and Thomas Aquinas, its origins go back to Plato,
Aristotle, and Cicero in ancient Greece and Rome. So it is a tradition, although it has been refined and enriched from Scripture.
Many non-Christians agree with its reasonableness, even though
they may not accept the authority of Scripture.

Again, we can occupy common ground with non-Christians
and join hands with them, in our desire both to protect human
rights and to preserve the natural environment. Respect for
human beings is a major concern of secular humanists, who are
dedicated to the human cause, even if their reasons differ from
those of Christians. As for conservation, it is possible to agree
about the unity of space-ship earth, the delicate balance of nature, our common dependence on air, water, and earth, and the
distinction between capital resources (like fossil fuels) and income—without ever quoting a text from Genesis 1 and 2 or from
any other part of Scripture.

My last example concerns the use of Sunday. The duty to safeguard one day in seven for worship and rest is laid down in the
fourth commandment, which is still in force. But we shall not secure Sunday observance merely by quoting God's law—or not
until people are converted. Meanwhile, however, we believe that
it is God's will to maintain this rhythm, that the nation is well
served by legislative protection of Sunday as a different day, that
family life is built up by it, that workers are thus protected
against being compelled to work, and that at least 'spectator

sports' (which demand the transportation of large numbers of people and the provision of policing, catering, fire and ambulance services) should be prohibited. For why should some people get their rest and recreation at the expense of others who have to work to provide it? And when the biblical argument is unacceptable, the historical argument may convince. Several attempts have been made to change the one-day-in-seven rhythm, either by cancelling the day of rest altogether or by lengthening the working week. For example, the French revolutionaries, after abolishing the monarchy and setting up the Republic in 1792, introduced a new republican calendar with a ten-day week. But the experiment survived only a few years. People could not last nine days without a break. So in 1805 Napoleon restored the seven-day week. Something similar happened after the Russian revolution a century later. In sweeping away religious institutions, the revolutionary leaders turned Sunday into a working day. But again it did not last, and Stalin restored Sunday as a day of rest.

We should not be unduly concerned that the arguments mentioned in nearly all my examples are drawn from self-interest. For when we are looking for reasoning which will appeal to the public at large, we have to be realistic. 'The art of government, in fact,' wrote William Temple, 'is the art of so ordering life that self-interest prompts what justice demands.'[16] People need to be convinced that the laws which govern their life are for their good, and that it is to their advantage to be law-abiding. This is even more true of groups than it is of individuals. Indeed, the main thesis of Reinhold Niebuhr's book *Moral Man and Immoral Society* is that, whereas 'individual men may be moral in the sense that they are able to consider interests other than their own in determining problems of conduct,' we have to recognise 'the brutal character of the behaviour of all human collectives, and the power of self-interest and collective egoism in all inter-group relations.'[17]

Political Systems

Social action is not only a question of winning the public debate, but of securing legislation which makes public life more pleasing to God. Not that every sin should be made a crime, and all duty buttressed by legal sanctions. For there are areas of private life into which the law should not intrude. For example, in Moslem countries private sexual immorality is a punishable offence, whereas in Christian countries it is not, unless it harms other people in some way. The main function of the law is to safeguard the accepted values of society and to protect the rights of citizens. Laws must also be enforceable, which means that they must enjoy public approval. To frame and pass such laws requires political power, and in a democracy majority power in Parliament or Congress.

It is no good saying that Jesus and his apostles were not interested in politics, and that they neither required nor even commended political action, let alone engaged in it themselves. It is true. They did not. But we have to remember that they were a tiny, insignificant minority under the totalitarian regime of Rome. The legions were everywhere, and were under orders to suppress dissent, crush opposition and preserve the status quo. The first century Christians *could* not take political action; is this the reason why they *did* not? At least the fact that they did not because they could not is no reason why we should not—if we can.

The question is: Would they have been politically active if they had had the opportunity to be and the likelihood of success? I believe they would. For without appropriate political action some social needs simply cannot be met. The apostles did not demand the abolition of slavery. But are we not glad and proud that nineteenth-century Christians did? Their campaign was based on biblical teaching regarding human dignity, and was a legitimate extrapolation from it. The apostles did not build hospitals either, or require them to be built, but Christian hospitals are a legitimate extrapolation from Jesus' compassionate concern for the sick. Just so, political action (which is love seeking justice for the oppressed) is a legitimate extrapolation from the teaching and ministry of Jesus.

What is necessary now is to take up the three alternative attitudes to social change which we have been considering and give them a political twist, at the same time noting what view of man each presupposes.

Absolutism is the political expression of 'imposition.' An absolutist government makes and enforces laws without the checks of a constitution or of consultation with the people. Absolutism arises from an entirely *pessimistic* view of human beings. Either they are thought to be too stupid to know what is good for them and for society, or, if they do know, then they cannot agree about it or they do not want it. In consequence, the argument runs, 'we have to tell 'em what's good for 'em; we'll knock their heads together and make 'em conform.' The public justification given is always that tight control is necessary for the sake of social order. And occasionally an autocracy has been genuinely benevolent. Nevertheless, it demeans citizens because it does not trust them to have any share in decision-making.

Anarchy could be regarded as the political expression of 'laissez-faire.' Not that it was in the nineteenth century, for its original advocates cherished the vision of an ordered society, with laissez-faire economics as the means to that end. But the modern laissez-faire attitude would naturally lead to the abolition of all government and law, and would arise from a naively *optimistic* view of human beings. It assumes that they are perfectly capable of governing themselves, and that laws are unnecessary to create a just society. 'Leave people alone,' it is said, 'and all will be well.'

So then, absolutism considers rigid control essential because it is pessimistic about man, denying his dignity due to his creation in God's image. Anarchy, on the other hand, considers unrestricted freedom safe because it is optimistic about man, denying his depravity due to the Fall. Both are politically mistaken because both are theologically mistaken, being based on false doctrines of man. They are also disastrous in practice. Absolutism leads to tyranny, not justice; and anarchy to chaos, not utopia.

Democracy is the third alternative. It is the political expression of 'persuasion by argument.' If absolutism being pessimistic imposes law arbitrarily, and anarchy being optimistic dispenses with law altogether, then democracy, being realistic about man as both created and fallen, involves citizens in the framing of their own laws. At least this is the theory. In practice, especially in countries with a large number of illiterates, the media can too easily manipulate them. And in every democracy there is the constant danger of trampling on minorities.

'The word "democracy" and its derivatives apply to decision-procedures,' writes John R. Lucas in his book *Democracy and Participation*. It describes three aspects of the decision-making process. The first concerns *who* takes it. 'A decision is democratically taken if the answer to the question "who takes it?" is "more or less everybody," in contrast to decisions taken only by those best qualified to take them, as in a meritocracy, or those taken by only one man, as in an autocracy or monarchy.' Secondly, democracy describes *how* a decision is reached. 'A decision is taken democratically if it is reached by discussion, criticism, and compromise.' Thirdly, democracy describes *the spirit* in which a decision is made, namely 'being concerned with the interests of all, instead of only a faction or a party.'[18]

So democracy reflects the balanced biblical view of man, as we might expect in view of its roots in post-Reformation Christian Europe. It also gives Christians the opportunity to make a constructive contribution in a pluralistic society, by getting into the public debate (whether on disarmament or divorce, abortion or *in vitro* fertilization) and by seeking to influence public opinion until there is a public demand for legislation which would be more pleasing to God. Democracy is government by consent, consent depends on consensus (or at least does so when electoral procedures are truly democratic), and consensus arises out of a discussion in which the issues become clarified.

Of course the democratic political process is also 'the art of the possible.' Because human beings are fallen, there is bound to be a gap between the divine ideal and the human reality, between what God has revealed and what man finds possible. Jesus himself recognized this distinction within the law of Moses. For Moses' permission of divorce in a case of 'indecency' or 'immorality' was given 'because your hearts were hard' (Mark 10.5). In other words, it was a concession to human weakness. But Jesus immediately added that 'from the beginning it was not so,' reminding them of the divine ideal.

There is a great need for more Christian thinkers in contemporary society, who will throw themselves into the public debate, and for more Christian activists who will organise pressure groups to promote the work of persuasion. Their motivation will be thoroughly Christian—a vision of the God who cares about justice, compassion, honesty, and freedom in society, and a vision of man, made in God's image though fallen, moral, responsible, with a conscience to be respected. It will be out of zeal for God and love for man that they will seek the renewal of society. They will make no attempt to conceal the origins of their concern. Yet in the parry and thrust of debate their arguments will often have to be *ad hominem,* and in the policies they develop they will have to be content with reality. And all the time, their goal will be the shaping of public opinion.

Addressing the need for Christians to live in cheerful protest against the assumptions of the consumer society, Bishop John V. Taylor of Winchester has written: 'It is in the area of public opinion that this battle has to be fought. Nothing can achieve the change of policies which our very salvation demands but a profound re-orientation of public opinion.' He went on to quote Reg Prentice, who said in 1972, when Minister of Overseas Development, that the only way to increase Britain's concern for Third World nations was the 'slow, hard grind of public education and political pressure within rich countries.' Bishop Taylor concluded that Christ's 'renewals and revolutions begin quietly, like faith itself. They start growing from one tiny seed, the staggering thought: *things don't have to be like this.* When that idea begins to trickle down into the structures and into the minds of ordinary people in our affluent society, the cry may at last go up: you're nothing but a pack of cards!'[19]

Chapter Four

Alienation: Have We Any Influence?

NO SINGLE WORD CAPTURES MORE ACCURATELY, OR EXPRESSES MORE eloquently, the modern sense of impotence than the word *alienation*. To say 'I'm alienated' means 'I can't relate to society any longer and, what's worse, I can't do anything about it.'

Marx popularised the term. But he was referring to an economic order in which the workers, because their products were sold by the factory owner, were thus alienated from the fruits of their labour. Contemporary Marxists give the word a broader application. Jimmy Reid, for example, a Communist councillor of Glasgow, Scotland, and chief spokesman of the Upper Clyde Shipyard Workers, said in 1972: 'Alienation is the cry of men who feel themselves to be the victims of blind economic forces beyond their control . . . , the frustration of ordinary people excluded from the processes of decision-making.'[1]

So alienation is the feeling of economic and political powerlessness. The juggernauts of institutionalised power roll ruthlessly on their way, and the common man or woman cannot do anything to change their direction or speed, let alone stop them. We are nothing but spectators of a developing situation which we feel helpless to influence in any way. That is 'alienation.'

95

In spite of my theological defence of democratic theory, and my plea that Christians should take advantage of the democratic process and join in the public debate, I have to admit that democracy does not always cure alienation, for many are disillusioned with its realities. It is this gulf between theory and practice which lies at the heart of John R. Lucas's book *Democracy and Participation*, from which I quoted in the last chapter. People exercise their democratic right to vote, and, to be sure, 'the vote constitutes a form of minimal participation' (p. 166). Thereafter, however, 'democracy becomes an autocracy, in which all decisions save one are taken by the autocrat, and the only decision left to the people is the occasional choice of autocrat.' So he renames democracy an 'elective autocracy,' because it 'enables people to participate in government only to a derisory extent.' It also 'makes the government singularly insensitive to the wishes of the governed and the requirements of justice' (p. 184). Again, 'although elective autocracy has its democratic aspect, it is deeply undemocratic as regards the way and the spirit in which decisions are taken. . . . It is non-participatory' (p. 198). Without doubt this disenchantment with the actual workings of democracy is widespread. Christians should share with others the concern to broaden the context of public debate, until parliamentary discussions 'reverberate in every inn and workshop in the realm.' Dr. Lucas ends his book with the delightful statement that 'democracy can flourish only in a land of pubs' (p. 264).

To me it is sad that many Christians become contaminated by the mood of alienation. 'To be sure,' they agree, 'the quest for social justice is our concern and we cannot escape this fact. But the obstacles are immense. Not only are the issues complex (we claim no expertise), but society is pluralistic (we claim no monopoly of power or privilege), and the forces of reaction dominate (we have no influence). The receding tide of Christian faith in the community has left us high and dry. In addition, human beings are selfish and society is rotten. It is entirely unrealistic to hope for social change.'

The first antidote to this mixture of secular alienation and Christian pessimism is history. History is full of examples of social change as a result of Christian influence. Take England as an example. Social progress, especially as a result of biblical Christianity, cannot be denied. Think of some of the features which marred the country only two hundred years ago. Criminal law was so harsh that about two hundred offences were punishable by death; it was justly named 'the Bloody Code.' Slavery and the slave trade were still being defended as legitimate, even respectable. Men were 'press-ganged' into the army and navy. No education or health care was provided for the masses. Smallpox killed more than ten percent of every generation. Travel by horse and coach was made perilous by highwaymen. Social feudalism imprisoned people in a rigid class system, and condemned millions to abject poverty. Conditions in prisons, factories, and mines were unbelievably inhuman. Only Anglicans were eligible to enter university or parliament, although a few dissenters got in through the practice of 'occasional conformity.' One is ashamed that only two centuries ago so much injustice tarnished Britain's national life.

But the social influence of Christianity has been worldwide. K. S. Latourette sums it up at the conclusion of his seven volume *History of the Expansion of Christianity*. He refers in glowing terms to the effects of the life of Christ through his followers: 'No life ever lived on this planet has been so influential in the affairs of men. . . . From that brief life and its apparent frustration has flowed a more powerful force for the triumphal waging of man's long battle than any other ever known by the human race. . . . Through it hundreds of millions have been lifted from illiteracy and ignorance, and have been placed upon the road of growing intellectual freedom and of control over their physical environment. It has done more to allay the physical ills of disease and famine than any other impulse known to man. It has emancipated millions from chattel slavery and millions of others from thraldom to vice. It has protected tens of millions from exploitation by their fellows. It has been the most fruitful source of movements to lessen the horrors of war and to put the relations of men and nations on the basis of justice and peace.'[2]

So Christian pessimism is historically unfounded. It is also theologically inept. We have seen that the Christian mind holds together the biblical events of creation, fall, redemption, and consummation. Christian pessimists concentrate on the fall ('human beings are incorrigible') and the consummation ('Christ is coming to put things right'), and imagine that these truths justify social despair. But they overlook the creation and the redemption. The divine image in mankind has not been obliterated. Human beings, though evil, can still do good, as Jesus plainly taught (Matthew 7.11). And the evidence of our eyes confirms it. There are non-Christian people who have good marriages, non-Christian parents who bring their children up well, non-Christian industrialists who run factories on a just basis, and non-Christian doctors who still take the Hippocratic standards as their guide and are conscientious in the care of their patients. This is partly because the truth of God's law is written on all human hearts, and partly because the values of God's kingdom, when embodied in the Christian community, are often recognised and to some extent imitated by people outside it. In this way the Gospel has borne fruit in western society over many generations. In addition, Jesus Christ redeems people and makes them new. Are we saying that regenerated and renewed people can do nothing to restrain or reform society? Such an opinion is monstrous. The combined witness of history and Scripture is that Christian people have had an enormous influence on society. We are not powerless. Things can be different. Nikolai Berdyaev summed the situation up admirably in these words: 'The sinfulness of human nature does not mean that social reforms and improvements are impossible. It only means that there can be no perfect and absolute social order . . . before the transfiguration of the world.'[3]

Salt and Light

From history and Scripture I turn to the expectation which Jesus had for his followers. He expressed it most vividly in the Sermon on the Mount by the use of the salt and light metaphors:

You are the salt of the earth. But if the salt loses its saltiness,
how can it be made salty again? It is no longer good for anything,
except to be thrown out and trampled by men.

You are the light of the world. A city on a hill cannot be hid-
den. Neither do people light a lamp and put it under a bowl. In-
stead they put it on its stand, and it gives light to everyone in the
house. In the same way, let your light shine before men, that they
may see your good deeds and praise your Father in heaven.

Matthew 5.13–16

Everybody is familiar with salt and light. They are found in
virtually every household in the world. Jesus himself, as a boy in
the Nazareth home, must often have watched his mother Mary
use salt in the kitchen and light the lamps when the sun went
down. He knew their practical usefulness.

So these were the images which Jesus later used to illustrate
the influence he expected his disciples to exert in human society.
At that time they were very few in number, the initial nucleus of
his new society; yet they were to be salt and light to the whole
earth. What did he mean? At least four truths cannot be missed:

First, *Christians are fundamentally different from non-Christians*, or
ought to be. Both images set the two communities apart. The
world is dark, Jesus implied, but you are to be its light. The
world is decaying, but you are to be its salt, and hinder its decay.
In English idiom we might say they are as different as 'chalk
from cheese' or 'oil from water'; Jesus said they are as different as
light from darkness, and salt from decay. This is a major theme
of the whole Bible. God is calling out from the world a people for
himself, and the vocation of this people is to be 'holy' or 'different.' 'Be holy,' he says to them again and again, 'because I am
holy.'

Secondly, *Christians must permeate non-Christian society*. Although
Christians are (or should be) morally and spiritually distinct
from non-Christians, they are not to be socially segregated. On
the contrary, their light is to shine into the darkness, and their
salt to soak into the decaying meat. The lamp does no good if it is
put under a bed or a bowl, and the salt does no good if it stays in

the salt cellar. Similarly, Christians are not to remain aloof from society, where they cannot affect it, but become immersed in its life. They are to let their light shine, so that their good deeds are seen.

Thirdly, *Christians can influence non-Christian society*. Before the days of refrigeration, salt was the best known preservative. Either it was rubbed into fish and meat, or they were left to soak in it. In this way the decaying process was retarded, though not of course entirely arrested. Light is even more obviously effective; when the light is switched on, the darkness is actually dispelled. Just so, Jesus seems to have meant, Christians can hinder social decay and dispel the darkness of evil. William Temple wrote of the 'pervasive sweetening of life and of all human relationships by those who carry with them something of the mind of Christ.'[4]

This prompts the question why Christians have not had a far greater influence for good on the non-Christian world. American friends will forgive me if I take the United States as my example, although in principle the situation is the same in Europe. The published statistics of American Christianity are staggering.

Christianity Today summarised the situation in these words at the end of 1979: 'Sixty-nine million Americans profess personal faith in Jesus Christ. Sixty-seven per cent of Americans today are church members. A recent Gallup Study determined that forty-four per cent of the public attend church frequently, and forty-five million Americans of fourteen years and older described themselves as "highly religious."'[5] Why then has this great army of Christian soldiers not been more successful in beating back the forces of evil? This is American futurologist Tom Sine's explanation: 'We have been remarkably effective at diluting his [sc. Christ's] extremist teaching and truncating his radical gospel. That explains why we can have a nation of 200 million people, 60 million of whom profess to be Christian, and yet make such an embarrassingly little difference in the morality of our society.'[6] More important than mere numbers of professing disciples are both the quality of their discipleship (maintaining Christ's standards without compromise) and their strategic deployment (capturing positions of influence for Christ). Our Christian habit is to bewail the world's deteriorating standards with an air of rather self-righteous dismay. We criticise its violence, dishonesty, immorality, disregard for human life, and materialistic greed.

'The world is going down the drain,' we say with a shrug. But whose fault is it? Who is to blame? Let me put it like this. If the house is dark when nightfall comes, there is no sense in blaming the house, for that is what happens when the sun goes down. The question to ask is 'where is the light?' If the meat goes bad and becomes inedible, there is no sense in blaming the meat, for that is what happens when the bacteria are left alone to breed. The question to ask is 'where is the salt?'

Just so, if society deteriorates and standards decline, till it becomes like a dark night or stinking fish, there is no sense in blaming society, for that is what happens when fallen men and women are left to themselves, and human selfishness is unchecked. The question to ask is 'where is the Church? Why are the salt and light of Jesus Christ not permeating and changing society?' It is sheer hypocrisy on our part to raise our eyebrows, shrug our shoulders or wring our hands. The Lord Jesus told *us* to be the world's salt and light. If therefore darkness and rottenness abound, it is our fault and we must accept the blame.

Fourthly, *Christians must retain their Christian distinctness.* If salt does not retain its saltness, it is good for nothing. If light does not retain its brightness, it becomes ineffective. So we who claim to be Christ's followers have to fulfil two conditions if we are to do any good for him. On the one hand we have to permeate non-Christian society, and immerse ourselves in the life of the world. On the other, while doing so, we have to avoid becoming assimilated to the world. We must retain our Christian convictions, values, standards, and life-style. We are back with the 'double identity' of the Church ('holiness' and 'worldliness') which I mentioned in the first chapter. Then, if it be asked what the 'saltiness' and 'brightness' of Christian holiness are, the rest of the Sermon on the Mount gives us the answer. For in it Jesus tells us not to be like others around us: 'do not be like them' (Matthew 6.8). Instead, he calls us to a greater righteousness (of the heart), a wider love (even of enemies), a deeper devotion (of children coming to their Father), and a nobler ambition (seeking first God's rule and righteousness).[7] It is only as we choose and follow his way, that our salt will retain its saltiness, our light will shine, we shall be his effective witnesses and servants, and exert a wholesome influence on society.

This purpose and expectation of Christ should be enough to overcome our sense of alienation. We may be ostracised by some at work or in our local community. Secular society may do its best to push us on to the circumference of its concerns. But, refusing to be marginalised, we should seek to occupy a sphere of influence for Christ. Ambition is the desire to succeed. There is nothing wrong with it if it is genuinely subordinated to the will and glory of God. True, power can corrupt. True also, the power of Christ is best displayed in our weakness. And indeed we shall continue to feel our personal inadequacy. Yet we should determine by his grace to infiltrate some secular segment of society and raise his flag there, maintaining without compromise his standards of love, truth, and goodness.

But how can we exert some influence for Christ? What does it mean in practice to be the world's salt and light? What can we do for social change? I will try to develop six ways, in three pairs.

Prayer and Evangelism

First, there is the power of prayer. I beg you not to dismiss this as a pious platitude, a sop to Christian convention. For it really is not. We cannot read the Bible without being impressed by its constant emphasis on the efficacy of prayer. 'The prayer of a righteous man is powerful and effective,' wrote James (5.16). 'I tell you,' said Jesus, 'that if two of you on earth agree about anything you ask for, it will be done for you by my Father in heaven' (Matthew 18.19). We do not claim to understand the rationale of intercession. But somehow it enables us to enter the field of spiritual conflict, and to align ourselves with the good purposes of

God, so that his power is released and the principalities of evil are bound.

Prayer is an indispensable part of the individual Christian's life. It is also indispensable to the life of the local church. Paul gave it priority: 'First of all, then, I urge that supplications, prayers, intercessions, and thanksgivings be made for all men, for kings and all who are in high positions, that we may lead a quiet and peaceable life, godly and respectful in every way. This is good, and it is acceptable in the sight of God our Saviour, who desires all men to be saved and to come to the knowledge of the truth' (1 Timothy 2.1–4 RSV).

Here is prayer for national leaders, that they may fulfil their responsibility to maintain conditions of peace, in which the Church is free both to obey God and to preach the gospel. In theory, we are convinced of this duty to pray. Yet some Christian social activists seldom stop to pray. And some churches hardly seem to take it seriously. If in the community (indeed, in the world) there is more violence than peace, more oppression than justice, more secularism than godliness, is it that Christians and churches are not praying as they should?

This is how the Church's obligation in this matter was expressed in the report of the international Consultation on the Relation between Evangelism and Social Responsibility (1982):

> We resolve ourselves, and call upon our churches, to take much more seriously the period of intercession in public worship; to think in terms of ten or fifteen minutes rather than five; to invite lay people to share in leading, since they often have deep insight into the world's needs; and to focus our prayers both on the evangelisation of the world [closed lands, resistant peoples, missionaries, national churches, etc.] and on the quest for peace and justice in the world [places of tension and conflict, deliverance from the nuclear horror, rulers and governments, the poor and needy, etc.]. We long to see every Christian congregation bowing down in humble and expectant faith before our Sovereign Lord.[8]

We also rejoice over the growth of parachurch movements whose goal is to stimulate the prayers of the people of God (e.g.

in the U.K. the Lydia Fellowship and Intercessors for Britain).

I turn now from the power of prayer to the power of the gospel, for our second Christian duty is evangelism. This book is about Christian social responsibility, not evangelism. Nevertheless, the two belong together. Although different Christians have received different gifts and callings, and although in some situations it is perfectly proper to concentrate on either evangelism or social action without combining them, nevertheless in general and in theory they cannot be separated. Our love for our neighbour will be fleshed out in a holistic concern for all his needs, of his body, soul, and community. That is why in the ministry of Jesus words and works were bracketed. As the Grand Rapids Report put it, evangelism and social activity are 'like the two blades of a pair of scissors or the two wings of a bird.'[9]

There are, however, two particular ways in which evangelism should be seen as a necessary prelude to and foundation of social action. The first is that the gospel changes people. Every Christian should be able to echo Paul's words with conviction: 'I am not ashamed of the gospel, because it is the power of God for the salvation of everyone who believes' (Romans 1.16). We know it in our lives, and we have seen it in the lives of others. If sin is at root self-centredness, then the transformation from 'self' to 'unself' is an essential ingredient of salvation. Faith leads to love, and love to service. So social activity, which is the loving service of the needy, should be the inevitable result of saving faith, although we have to confess that this is not always so.

There are other situations in which positive social change is taking place apart from explicit Christian initiatives. So we must not bind evangelism and social change together so indissolubly as to say that the former *always* issues in the latter and the latter *never* happens without the former. Nevertheless, these are exceptions which prove the rule. We still insist that evangelism is the major instrument of social change, for the gospel changes people, and changed people can change society. We have seen that society needs salt and light; but only the gospel can create them. This is one way in which we may declare without embarrassment that evangelism takes primacy over social action. Logically speaking, 'Christian social responsibility presupposes socially responsible Christians,' and it is the gospel which produces them.[10]

When John V. Taylor, Bishop of Winchester, was still General Secretary of the Church Missionary Society, he described in his *CMS Newsletter* (May 1972) his reactions to Geoffrey Moorhouse's book *Calcutta*, and indeed to the apparent hopelessness of that city's problems. 'But invariably what tips the balance from despair to faith,' he wrote, 'is the person who rises above the situation.' Such persons are neither 'trapped' in the city, nor have they 'escaped' from it. 'They have *transcended* the situation. . . . Salvation is not the same as solution: it precedes it and makes it a possibility. . . . Personal salvation—salvation in first gear—is still the way in. It is the key to unlock the door of determinism and make possible the "salvation" of corporate organisations and institutions—salvation in second gear—by providing those who can transcend the situation.'

There is another way in which social uplift is facilitated by evangelism. When the gospel is faithfully and widely preached, it not only brings a radical renewal to individuals, but produces what Raymond Johnston has called 'an antiseptic atmosphere,' in which blasphemy, selfishness, greed, dishonesty, immorality, cruelty, and injustice find it harder to flourish. A country which has been permeated by the gospel is not a soil in which these poisonous weeds can take root, let alone luxuriate.

More than this. The gospel which changes people also changes cultures. One of the greatest hindrances to social change is the conservatism of culture. A country's laws, institutions, and customs have taken centuries to develop; they have a built-in resistance to reform. In some cases, the moral ambiguity of culture is the hindrance. Every political programme, economic system, and development plan depends on values to motivate and sustain it. It cannot operate without honesty and some degree of altruism. So progress is effectively blocked if the national culture (and the religion or ideology which shapes it) connives at corruption and

selfishness, and offers no incentive to self-control or self-sacrifice. Then culture stands in the way of development.

Professor Brian Griffiths applied this principle with great insight to both Capitalism and Marxism in his 1980 London Lectures in Contemporary Christianity, *Morality and the Market Place.*
To him Capitalism has lost its legitimacy and Marxism is fatally
flawed. 'Capitalism suffers because of inadequate limits on the
exercise of freedom,' while Communism 'suffers from an inability to put adequate constraints on the urge to control.' But this
'inability to resolve the basic tension between freedom and control' is the crisis of secular humanism. Both Capitalism and
Marxism are, in fact, the product of the eighteenth-century En-
lightenment: what they lack is Christian values.[11]

Brian Griffiths' last chapter is entitled 'Third World Poverty
and First World Responsibility.' He takes issue with a key expression used by Herr Willy Brandt in his Introduction to the
Brandt Commission Report: 'We take it for granted that all cultures deserve equal respect, protection and promotion.'[12] 'But
they do not,' is Brian Griffiths' rejoinder. 'Cultures express values
which shape institutions and motivate people—some of which
. . . promote wealth and justice and liberty, and others of which
do not.'[13]

It is entirely logical, therefore, that a book on economics, and
in particular on *Morality and the Market Place,* should conclude
with a passionate plea for world evangelism. 'Christianity starts
with faith in Christ and it finishes with service in the world. . . .
Because of this I believe that evangelism has an indispensable
part to play in the establishment of a more just economic order.
Obedience to Christ demands change, the world becomes his
world, the poor, the weak and the suffering are men, women and
children created in his image; injustice is an affront to his creation; despair, indifference and aimlessness are replaced by
hope, responsibility and purpose; and above all selfishness is
transformed by love.'[14]

So the gospel changes both people and cultures. This is not to
say that no development is possible without evangelism, but

rather that development is hindered without, and greatly facilitated by, the cultural changes which the gospel brings. And the more the gospel spreads, the more hopeful the situation becomes. Even a few Christians in public life can initiate social change. But their influence is likely to be far greater if they have massive grassroots support, as the nineteenth-century British evangelical reformers did. So Christians in every country should pray for a widespread acceptance of the gospel. As the nineteenth-century American evangelicals clearly saw, revival and reform belong together.

Witness and Protest

We have seen that the gospel is God's power for salvation. But in fact all truth is powerful. God's truth is much more mighty than the devil's crooked lies. We should never be afraid of the truth. Nor do we ever need to be afraid *for* the truth, as if its survival hung in the balance. For God watches over it and will never allow it to be completely suppressed. As Paul put it, 'we cannot do anything against the truth, but only for the truth' (2 Corinthians 13.8). And as John put it, 'the light shines in the darkness, but the darkness has not overcome it' (John 1.5, margin).

One contemporary Christian thinker who is convinced about this is Solzhenitsyn. His Nobel Speech on Literature (1970) was entitled *One Word of Truth*. He confessed that writers lack all material weapons like rockets and tanks. So 'what can literature do,' he asked, 'in the face of the merciless onslaught of open violence?' First, it can refuse 'to take part in the lie.' Secondly, writers and artists can 'vanquish the lie.' For *one word of truth outweighs the whole world*. And on such a fantastic breach of the law of conservation of mass and energy are based my own activities and my appeal to the writers of the world.'[15]

All Christians are called like their Master 'to bear witness to the truth.' This, he added, was why he had been born and why he had come into the world (John 18.37). The supreme truth to which we testify is of course Jesus Christ himself, for he is the truth (John 14.6). But all truth—scientific, biblical, theological, moral—is his, and we are to be fearless in defending, maintaining, and arguing it. This is the place for developing an ethical apologetic, as I was urging in the last chapter, and for entering into the public debate of contemporary issues. From the pulpit (still a much more influential 'platform' than is commonly realised, especially in the shaping of public opinion), through letters to and articles in national and local newspapers, in discussions at home and work, through opportunities on radio and television, by poetry and popular songs, we are called as Christians to witness to God's law and God's gospel, without fear or apology. Moreover, as with Jesus so with his followers, the true witness (*martus*) must be prepared to suffer, and even if necessary die, for his testimony. Such costly testimony is the chief weapon of those who are denied the democratic process because they live under an oppressive regime.

In a much-publicised speech about ten years ago, Sir Keith Joseph spoke about the moral decline of Britain, the possibility of 're-moralising' the nation, and the power of ideas. 'Are we to be destroyed from inside?' he asked, although we had repelled successive attempts at invasion from outside by Philip of Spain, Napoleon, the Kaiser, and Hitler. 'Are we to be destroyed by ideas, mischievous, wrongheaded, debilitating, yet seductive because they are fashionable and promise so much on the cheap?' Later in the speech he answered his own questions, and urged his listeners to go on to the offensive. 'We must fight the battle of ideas,' he cried, 'in every school, university, publication, committee, TV studio, even if we have to struggle for our toe-hold there. We have the truth. If we fail to make it shine clear, we shall be to blame no less than the exploiters, the casuists and the commercialisers.'[16]

Alongside a positive witness to the truth must go its negative counterpart, protest against folly, deceit, and wickedness. Many seem to be disenchanted with the weapon of rational protest, but I think they should not be. Public agitation is an effective weapon. It so happens that, while I am writing this chapter in 1983, several recent examples have come to my notice.

First, before this year's General Election, when William Whitelaw as Home Secretary published details of the Police and Criminal Evidence Bill which he intended to introduce into Parliament, there was an immediate outcry against its Clause 10, which would have given police the power to search for and remove confidential records held by clergymen, doctors, and social workers. Vigorous protests were made by lawyers and doctors, and fifty-five Church of England bishops signed a petition. Almost at once the Home Secretary announced that he would amend the Clause.

My second example comes from West Germany. When details of the 1983 population census were published, and it became known that respondents would be required to divulge a great deal of private information about themselves, there was a groundswell of protest. A law student and two lawyers used the right of German citizens, when they believe that their civil liberties are being threatened, to appeal to the highest court of the land, the Federal Constitutional Court in Karlsruhe. The Court stopped the census, by what was virtually an interim injunction, in order to give them time to study its legality in full.

Thirdly, in July 1983 Britain's General Medical Council, reflecting policies of the Department of Health and Social Security, issued an instruction that doctors must 'observe the rules of professional secrecy' if a girl under sixteen insists that her parents should not be told that a contraceptive pill or an abortion has been prescribed for her, and that doctors refusing to respect such a girl's wishes would probably be disciplined, and might even be struck off the register. To be sure, there are exceptional circumstances (e.g. a history of parental violence) in which a child should be able to confide in her doctor. But the GMC's general ruling, which would have disposed altogether of the parents' right of consent, aroused enormous pressure from outraged doctors, parents, and church people, and the GMC climbed down.

Examples could be multiplied. Let no one say that protest is a waste of time and effort.

Example and Groups

Truth is powerful when it is argued; it is even more powerful when it is exhibited. For people need not only to understand the argument, but to see its benefits displayed. One Christian nurse in a hospital, teacher in a school, secretary in an office, assistant in a shop, or worker in a factory, can have an influence out of all proportion to numbers and percentages. And who can calculate the influence for good in the whole neighbourhood of a single Christian home, in which husband and wife are faithful to and find fulfilment in each other, their children grow up in the disciplined security of love, and the family are not turned in on themselves but outgoing to the community? Christians are marked people both at work and at home; the world is watching us.

More influential even than the example of Christian individuals and families is that of the local church. For the church is meant by God to be God's new and redeemed community, which embodies the ideals of his Kingdom. We must not underestimate, writes Dr. John Howard Yoder, 'the powerful . . . impact on society of the creation of an alternative social group.' For 'the primary social structure through which the gospel works to change other structures is that of the Christian community.'[17]

But how does the new community change the old? The answer is well-expressed in the *Grand Rapids Report*:

> *First, the new community should constitute a challenge to the old. Its values and ideals, its moral standards and relationships, its sacrificial life-style, its love, joy and peace—these are the signs of the Kingdom . . . and present the world with a radically alternative society. . . .*
>
> *Secondly, as the world lives alongside the Kingdom community, some of the values of the Kingdom spill over into society as a whole, so that its industry, commerce, legislation and institutions become to some degree imbued with Kingdom values. So-called 'Kingdomized' or 'Christianized' society is not the Kingdom of God, but it owes a debt to the Kingdom which often is unrecognized.*

The 'overspill' model has its limitations, however, because it pictures the two communities as independent of one another, like two vessels standing side by side, the contents of one spilling over into the other. The salt, light and yeast metaphors which Jesus employed are more dynamic, since each implies the penetration of the old community by the new.[18]

Small groups of Christian people can be visible embodiments of the gospel. They can also make use of all the means of influencing society which I have mentioned so far. There is power in prayer and in the gospel; there is even more if we pray and evangelise together. There is power in witness and protest; there is even more if we testify and take action together. The group was our Lord's own chosen way. He began with the Twelve. And the long history of the Church abounds in examples of the strategic influence of small groups.

In sixteenth-century Cambridge the early Reformers met in the White Horse Inn to study Erasmus's Greek New Testament; in eighteenth-century Oxford the Holy Club, to which the Wesleys and Whitefield belonged, although engaged in barren good works, was the background against which the first evangelical revival began; and in nineteenth-century London the Clapham Sect gave their support to Wilberforce in his anti-slavery campaign and to many other social and religious causes.

Today one of the most promising features of modern church life is the hunger for the small group experience. Quite apart from the independent House Church movement, thousands of congregations have divided their membership into small fellowship or home groups. Many churches also encourage the formation of specialist groups—evangelistic visiting teams, missionary prayer groups, music groups, contemporary issues groups, reading groups, social study and action groups. The number is almost endless.

Then there are communities experimenting in new styles of living, sharing and/or working together; for example, the Kairos Community in Buenos Aires (for theological reflection on discipleship in the secular world), the Sojourners Community in Washington D.C. (involved in producing *Sojourners* magazine which promotes a concern for peace and justice, and in serving local Black families), and TRACI in New Delhi (The Research and Communication Institute of young Indian thinkers and writers). And in Britain there are groups like the Shaftesbury Project (encouraging research and action related to Christian involvement in society), CARE Trust (Christian Action Research and Education, promoting moral standards in society), and I might mention the London Institute for Contemporary Christianity (promoting the integration of discipleship under Christ's Lordship and the penetration of the secular world for him).

A widely respected Roman Catholic leader who believes strongly in the potential of small groups is Dom Helder Camara, Archbishop of Recife in northeast Brazil. Accused of being subversive, forbidden access to the media, under constant threat of assassination, this 'violent peacemaker' (as he has been called) is committed to justice and peace. Having travelled half the world for several years, appealing to institutions, he now puts more faith in groups. He encourages the formation of 'Abrahamic minorities' (so-called 'because like Abraham we are hoping against hope')[19] in neighbourhoods, university and unions, within the media, in management, among politicians and in the armed forces. Sharing a common thirst for justice and freedom, they gather information; they try to diagnose the problems relating to housing, unemployment, sweated labour, structures; they pool experiences and take whatever action of 'peaceful violence' they deem appropriate.

Dom Helder believes that such minority groups have 'the power for love and justice which could be likened to nuclear energy locked for millions of years in the smallest atoms and waiting to be released.'[20] 'All these minorities united could become an irresistible force,' he adds.[21] Some ridicule him, but he perseveres. 'My plan, I am well aware,' he has written, 'may call to mind the combat against Goliath. But the hand of God was with the young shepherd, and David conquered the Philistine with his

faith, a sling and five small stones.'[22] 'Keep in mind,' he urges
elsewhere, 'that throughout the centuries humanity has been led
by daring minorities.'[23]

This contrast between the giant and the boy, the sword and the
slingstones, arrogant boasting and humble trust, is characteristic
of God's activity in the world. Tom Sine has captured it well in
his book *The Mustard Seed Conspiracy*, whose title alludes to the
tiny seed out of which a large bush grows. Its subtitle is 'You can
make a difference in tomorrow's troubled world.' He writes:
'Jesus let us in on an astonishing secret. God has chosen to
change the world through the lowly, the unassuming and the
imperceptible. . . . That has always been God's strategy—changing the world through the conspiracy of the insignificant. He
chose a ragged bunch of Semite slaves to become the insurgents
of his new order. . . . And who would have ever dreamed that
God would choose to work through a baby in a cow stall to turn
the world right side up! "God chose the foolish things . . . the
weak things . . . the lowly things . . . the things that are not. . . ."
It is still God's policy to work through the embarrassingly insignificant to change his world and create his future. . . .'[24]

'The embarrassingly insignificant.' I feel the need to underline
this topsy-turvy policy which God has adopted. At the same
time, I am anxious we should grasp that it is realistic. What minorities lack in numbers, they can make up in conviction and
commitment. For support of this contention I call on the witness
of a well-known American sociologist. Robert Bellah is a specialist in 'civil religion,' and in the influence of religion and ethics on
politics. He lectures in the Department of Sociology at the University of California, Berkeley, and also in its Center for Japanese
and Korean Studies. In an interview with Sam Keen in *Psychology
Today* (January 1976), he said: 'I think we should not underestimate the significance of the small group of people who have a
new vision of a just and gentle world. In Japan a very small minority of Protestant Christians introduced ethics into politics,
and had an impact beyond all proportion to their numbers. They
were central in beginning the women's movement, labor unions,

socialist parties, and virtually every reform movement. The quality of a culture may be changed when two percent of its people have a new vision.'

Christians are less than one percent in Japan, but many more than two percent in a large number of countries. We could have an enormous influence on society, in terms of both evangelism and social action, for the glory of God. There is simply no ground for a sense of alienation.

Part II

Global Issues

Chapter Five

The Nuclear Threat

OF ALL THE GLOBAL PROBLEMS WHICH CONFRONT THE HUMAN RACE today none is graver than the threat of a nuclear holocaust. War has always been horrible, whether fought by sticks and stones, bows and arrows, swords and spears, muskets and rifles, or bayonets and bombs. But in the case of these so-called 'conventional' weapons, there has been the possibility of controls and limits, and war has involved an engagement between armies. The arrival of the nuclear age, however, has rendered most military traditions obsolete. 'The unleashed power of the atom,' said Albert Einstein, 'has changed everything save our modes of thinking; and thus we are drifting towards unparalleled catastrophe. . . . A new type of thinking is essential if mankind is to survive.'[1] He was not exaggerating. Now that we have the power to destroy the total legacy of past civilisations, the present delicate ecological balance of the biosphere, and through radiation the genetic potential of the future, the very survival of the human race and of our planet is at stake.

Contemporary Realities

The Christian mind cannot operate in a vacuum. However strongly we hold fast to God's once-for-all revelation of himself in Christ and Scripture, we have to struggle to relate this to the harsh realities of the contemporary world. Thus revelation and reality belong together as we seek to discern God's will.

(1) The Arms Race

The NATO and Warsaw Pact countries together have more than twelve million in their armed forces. It is estimated that the two superpowers possess between them at least 15,000 'strategic' (intercontinental) and 27,000 'tactical' (short-range or battlefield) nuclear weapons. These nearly 50,000 warheads (some think nearly 60,000) are said to have a destructive power more than one million times greater than the Hiroshima bomb. Each Trident II submarine, which is replacing Poseidon and Polaris, will have the capacity to carry twenty-four missles, each with between eight and fourteen (according to range) independently-targeted warheads, each of which is twelve times more powerful than the Hiroshima bomb, so that together they could reach between 192 and 336 independent targets. Thus a single Trident II submarine will have the destructive equivalent of between 2,304 and 4,032 Hiroshima bombs.[2] Yet fourteen Tridents are on order. Moreover the SALT II agreement, even if it had been ratified, would only have set a ceiling to the number and type of missiles; the multiplication of warheads would have been unlimited.

The horrendous 'overkill' capacity of these nuclear arsenals appalls modern commentators. George Kennan, for example, the American expert in Soviet affairs, in his acceptance speech on receiving the Albert Einstein Peace Prize in Washington in May 1981, said that the nuclear nations were 'like the victims of some sort of hypnotism, like men in a dream, like lemmings heading for the sea.' The Soviet and American stockpiles, he went on, 'are simply fantastically redundant to the purpose in question.' So he called for a 'bold and sweeping' initiative, namely 'an immediate across-the-board reduction by fifty percent of the nuclear arsenals now being maintained by the two Superpowers,' with adequate verification procedures. But his cry went unheeded.

(2) Arms Expenditure

In order to grasp the scale of the manufacture of armaments, we have to consider not their quantity only, but their cost. The percentage of Gross National Product devoted to defence in 1982 was about 5 percent in the UK, 6 percent in the USA, 9 percent in the USSR (though some western estimates put it at twice this figure), and much higher in some Third World countries. In 1982 'together the nations of the world spent the equivalent of about 650 billion dollars on their armed forces each year.' This is 'more than one-twentieth of their total annual incomes.'[3] It is also more than one million dollars a minute.

President Eisenhower once said: 'Every gun that is made, every warship launched, every rocket fired, signifies . . . a theft from those who hunger and are not fed, from those who are cold and are not clothed.'[4] Although his concept of 'theft' may have been more rhetoric than economic reality, he was expressing his sense of outrage over the disparity between expenditure on arms and expenditure on development. What then would he have said about the nuclear arsenals of today? How should we correlate the thousands of millions spent on arms with the 800 million people in the world who are destitute?

(3) Nuclear Proliferation

Five nations are at present known to have nuclear weapons and delivery systems—the United States, the USSR, Britain, France and China. Nine more are known to have the capability to develop them—Argentina, West Germany, the Netherlands, Japan, India, Israel, South Africa, Pakistan, and Egypt. Others which have nuclear expertise and are sometimes called 'threshold countries,' include Brazil, Iraq, Libya, South Korea, and Taiwan. That makes nineteen nations. Many are warning that this number may soon double to thirty-five or forty, while by the year 2000 the 'nuclear club' may have more than doubled its membership again to nearly one hundred. Fred C. Ikle, Director of the Arms Control and Disarmament Agency, is quoted as having referred in 1975 to 'the inevitable worldwide spread of nuclear technology.'[5] The growing use of nuclear energy increases this risk, as well as the risk of nuclear accidents.

(4) The Consequences of Nuclear War

Probably nothing can bring home to us the ghastly effects of a nuclear explosion more vividly than the eye-witness accounts of what happened at Hiroshima and Nagasaki. Lord Mountbatten quoted one shortly before he was himself killed by an act of senseless violence:

> *Suddenly a glaring whitish, pinkish light appeared in the sky accompanied by an unnatural tremor which was followed almost immediately by a wave of suffocating heat and a wind which swept away everything in its path. Within a few seconds the thousands of people in the streets in the centre of the town were scorched by a wave of searing heat. Many were killed instantly, others lay writhing on the ground screaming in agony from the intolerable pain of their burns. Everything standing upright in the way of the blast . . . was annihilated. . . . Hiroshima had ceased to exist.*[6]

That was the result of a single, smallish atomic explosion. What the consequences of a nuclear war would be like it is impossible to predict with accuracy because of the many imponderables such as the number of warheads used, the distribution of people in the target zone, the degree of civil defence available, and the climatic conditions at the time. But the United States' Congress document *The Effects of Nuclear War* (1979) says that 'the minimum consequences would be enormous' and gives four escalating case studies.

A single megaton weapon attack on a single big city like Detroit or Leningrad would mean up to two million dead and a further one million injured. 'A very large attack against a range of military and economic targets,' in which the USSR struck first and the USA retaliated, would mean up to seventy-seven percent of the American population dead (160 million people) and up to forty percent of the Russian population (being more scattered in rural areas). These casualties would be the immediate effects (within the first thirty days) of the heat, blast, wind, fire storm, and direct radiation. Many more millions would die of their injuries (since the medical facilities would be completely inadequate), and of epidemics (due to the breakdown of sewerage and the non-availability of clean water),' or would starve or freeze to death during the first winter (because of the chaos of services). A pall of sooty toxic smoke over the devastated area would not only poison many survivors but so completely blot out the warmth and light of the sun as to return the earth to Ice Age conditions. In the long term cancer would claim many more victims, and both the genetic consequences and ecological devastation would continue for decades and be incalculable.[7]

Theological and Moral Reflections

Although Christians do not agree, and probably have never agreed, about the mind of Christ on war, yet we should neither exaggerate the disagreement between us nor minimize the substantial area in which we are at one. For example, all Christian people affirm that the Kingdom of God inaugurated by Jesus is God's rule of righteousness and peace; that Jesus himself perfectly exemplified in his conduct the ideals of the Kingdom he proclaimed; that the Kingdom community is to hunger for righteousness, to pursue peace, to forbear revenge, to love enemies, in other words to be marked by the Cross; and that in the consummated Kingdom ('they will beat their swords into ploughshares and their spears into pruning hooks,' for 'nation will not take up sword against nation, nor will they train for war any more' (Isaiah 2.4). All this must mean that, as Christians, we are primarily committed to peace and righteousness. True, the quest for peace with justice is much more costly than appeasement. We also admire the loyalty, self-sacrifice and courage of serving soldiers. Yet we must not glamourise or glorify war in itself, however just we may perceive its cause to be. Some Christians believe that in some circumstances it may be defended as the lesser of two evils, but it could never be regarded by the Christian mind as more than a painful necessity in a fallen world.

Apart from this general biblical background, however, there

are three main positions which Christians hold and defend—
total pacifism, the just war theory, and relative (or nuclear) pacifism.

(1) The Total Pacifist Position[8]

Pacifists tend to begin with the Sermon on the Mount. At least it
is from this part of the teaching of Jesus that many develop their
commitment to nonviolence. We are not to resist an evil person,
Jesus said. Instead, if he strikes us on the right cheek, we are to
turn to him the other also. We are to love our enemies, do good
to those who hate us and pray for those who persecute us. Only
so can we qualify as children of our Heavenly Father, for his love
is indiscriminate, and he gives the blessings of rain and sunshine
to the evil and the good alike. To hate those who love us is the
devil's way. To love those who love us and hate those who hate
us is the way of the world. If we would follow Jesus, however,
and accept the standards of his Kingdom, we must love those
who hate us (Matthew 5.38–48; Luke 6.27–36).

Moreover, Jesus practised what he preached. He exemplified
his call to nonresistance, for he resisted neither betrayal nor arrest, neither trial nor sentence, neither torture nor crucifixion.
When he was insulted, he did not retaliate. He was the innocent
suffering Servant of the Lord. 'He was led like a lamb to the
slaughter, and as a sheep before her shearers is silent, so he did
not open his mouth' (Isaiah 53.7). He loved those who despised
and rejected him. He even prayed for the forgiveness of those
who nailed him to the cross.

Thus, pacifists conclude, the teaching and example of Jesus together commit us to the way of nonresistance and nonviolence.
For this is the way of the Cross, and Jesus calls us to take up our
cross and follow him. Moreover, it seems to be historically
proven that for two centuries, until the conversion of Constan-
tine, the great majority of Christians refused to serve as soldiers.
There is clear evidence that their refusal related to the idolatrous
practices associated with life in the Roman army. Pacifists argue
that they also perceived war to be incompatible with their Christian obedience. This is not certain.

The pacifist position was adopted by the so-called 'Radical Reformers' of the sixteenth century (the various Anabaptist groups), is preserved by the 'Peace Churches' today (Quakers, Mennonites, United Brethren, etc.), and is also held by considerable minorities in the 'historic' Reformation churches.

(2) The 'Just War' Tradition[9]

The concept of the 'just war' antedates the Christian era and may be traced back both to the 'holy wars' of the Old Testament and to some Greek and Roman ethical teaching. The notion was Christianised by Augustine in the fourth century, however, systematised by Thomas Aquinas in the thirteenth, further developed by Francisco de Vitoria in the sixteenth, and endorsed by most of the Reformers. It is held by a majority of Roman Catholics and Protestants today.

It has been stated in various forms, although usually seven conditions have been specified, namely formal declaration, last resort, just cause, right intention, proportionate means, noncombatant immunity and reasonable expectation. There is some overlap in these seven criteria, however, and I find it more helpful to reduce them to three, relating to the beginning, the conduct, and the end of a war. Thus, for a war to be 'just,' first, *its cause must be righteous.* It must be defensive, not aggressive. Its objective must be to secure justice or remedy injustice, to protect the innocent or champion human rights. It must be undertaken as a last resort only, after all attempts at negotiation and reconciliation have been exhausted, and then only after a formal declaration (following an ultimatum) by a legitimate authority, not by groups or individuals. Moreover, the intention must be as righteous as the cause. Just causes are not served by unjust motives. So there must be no hatred, no animosity, no thirst for revenge.

Secondly, *its means must be controlled.* There must be no wanton or unnecessary violence. In fact two key words are used to describe the legitimate use of violence in a just cause. One is 'proportionate' and the other 'discriminate.' 'Proportionate' signifies that the war is perceived as the lesser of two evils, that the violence inflicted is proportionately less than that which it is intended to remedy, and that the ultimate gains will outweigh the losses. 'Discriminate' means that the war is directed against enemy combatants and military targets, and that civilians are immune. We have to concede that the total immunity of non-combatants is impossible to preserve. But in a 'just war' the distinction must be preserved and the *intentional* killing of civilians outlawed. The principle of noncombatant immunity was implicit in the Hague Conventions (1899 and 1907), became explicit in the Geneva Conventions and their Additional Protocol (1949 and 1977), and has been emphatically reaffirmed by the General Assembly of the United Nations (1970).

Thirdly, *its outcome must be predictable.* That is, like the king in Jesus' little parable who 'counted the cost' before going to war (Luke 14.31, 32), there must be a calculated prospect of victory, and so of achieving the just cause for which the war was begun.

To sum up, a 'just war' is one fought for a righteous cause, by controlled means, with a reasonable expectation of success.

The 'just war' theory is only a tradition, however. Can it be commended from Scripture? Some try to do so on the basis of the wars commanded and directed by Yahweh in the Old Testament. But this is a precarious procedure, since these were expressly sanctioned, and no nation can claim today to enjoy Israel's privileged position as a 'holy nation,' God's special covenant people, a unique theocracy.

A more secure basis is provided by Paul's teaching about the state in Romans 13.1–7, and its context. This is actually embedded in a passage about neighbour-love, since it is preceded by injunctions to love and serve our enemies (12.14–21) and followed by statements that love never harms our neighbour (13.8–10). We are therefore confronted by a different exegetical problem. In particular, the end of Romans 12 and the beginning of Romans 13 appear to be in conflict with one another. The first, echoing the Sermon on the Mount, forbids us to repay anybody evil for evil; the second, echoing rather the Old Testament, describes the state as God's agent for the punishment of evildoers. The first says that evildoers are to be served; the second that they are to be punished. How can these instructions be reconciled?

The Peace Churches tend to say that the requirement to love our enemies is primary, that the state's judicial function is incompatible with it, and that therefore the Christian community must keep aloof from the state, and have no share in its work.

A recent and eloquent advocate of this view is Dale Aukerman in his book *Darkening Valley*, 'a biblical perspective on nuclear war.' He cannot accept that God 'ordained' or 'instituted' the state ('God does not consecrate and hallow the civil authorities; such hallowing is reserved for the Messianic community'),[10] or that the state could be God's minister, except in a secondary sense. He uses two analogies. As in a collapsing marriage husband and wife accuse each other, and 'each is for the other God's agent of retribution,' though God is not the author of their quarrel, and as the Assyrian and Babylonian empires were agents of God's judgment, though God was not the author of their arrogant cruelty, so the violence of the civil authorities is not God's intention, yet 'they *are assigned* by God *a place* . . . , a role in the realm of his wrath.' This is his conclusion: 'Civil authorities in bearing the sword, which represents rule by threatened or inflicted violence, are sinning, going contrary to God's way of love described in the verses immediately before and after the Romans 13.1–7 parenthesis. . . . But in the retributive dynamisms that emerge under God as he sets himself against sin, civil authorities do have their place along with Assyria and the nagging wife.'[11]

This exegesis is open to serious criticism, however. The apostle Paul asserts that the governing authorities have been established by God, that he has delegated his authority to them, that therefore in submitting to them we are submitting to him and in rebelling against them we are rebelling against him. Further, 'the one in authority' (any official of the state) is 'God's servant' to reward the good citizen and punish the evildoer. In fact, three times Paul repeats that the state's 'authority' is God's authority and three times that the state's 'ministry' is God's ministry (verses 4a, 4b, and 6).

It seems clear to me that these are not grudging concessions that God has 'assigned a place' to the state, which when using force to punish evil is nevertheless 'sinning,' but genuine affirmations that God has 'established' the state with his authority and that when exercising its authority to punish evil it is doing God's will. This being so, I cannot see that Christian people should remain insulated from public life; they should rather involve themselves in it, knowing that in doing so they are 'ministers of God' just as much as pastors to whom the same expression is applied. There is nothing anomalous about Christians serving in the police force or the prison service, as politicians or magistrates or town councillors. For Christians worship a God who is just and are therefore committed to the quest for justice. The Christian community should not stand aloof from the secular community, but seek to penetrate it for Christ.

Among those who accept the legitimacy of Christian participation in the work of the secular authority are most pacifists who are not members of the Peace Churches. But, like all other Christians, they regard their participation as critical and conditional. For example, they would refuse to obey the state's call to take up arms.

How then should we resolve the apparent discrepancy between Romans 12.17–21 with its call for the loving service of enemies and Romans 13.1–7 with its call for the punishment of evildoers? We shall begin to perceive the answer when we notice that the contrast between forgiveness and punishment is not only *between* these paragraphs but embedded *within* the first. For the prohibition 'do not repay anyone evil for evil' is followed by 'I will repay, says the Lord' and the prohibition 'do not take revenge, my friends' is followed by 'leave room for God's wrath, for it is written: "It is mine to avenge"' (verses 17, 19). So the reason why wrath, revenge, and retribution are forbidden us is not because they are in themselves wrong reactions to evil, but because they are *God's* prerogative, not ours. Similarly Jesus himself, when 'they hurled insults at him,' not only 'did not retaliate' but also and instead 'entrusted himself [and his cause] to him who judges justly' (1 Peter 2.23).

It is better, then, to see the end of Romans 12 and the beginning of Romans 13 as complementary to one another. Members of God's new community can be both private individuals and state officials. In the former role we are never to take personal revenge or repay evil for evil, but rather bless our persecutors (12.14), serve our enemies (12.20), and seek to overcome evil with good (12.21). In the latter role, however, if we are called by God to serve as police or prison officers or judges, we are God's agents in the punishment of evildoers. True, 'vengeance' and 'wrath' belong to God, but one way in which he executes his judgment on evildoers today is through the state.

To 'leave room for God's wrath' (12.19) means to allow the state to be 'an agent of wrath to bring punishment on the wrongdoer' (13.4). This is not to say that the administration of justice should not be tempered with mercy. It should. And state officials should be concerned not only to 'punish' evil but to 'overcome' it, since retributive and reformative justice should go hand in hand. Nevertheless, what this passage of Scripture emphasises is that, if evil is to be punished (as it deserves to be), then the punishment must be administered by the state and its officials, and not by individuals who take the law into their own hands.[12]

It should be clear, then, that the state's punishing role is strictly limited and controlled. There is no possible justification in Romans 13.1–7 for an oppressive regime to whom the words 'law and order' have become a synonym for tyranny. No. The state is God's agent to execute his wrath only on evildoers, that is, on particular and identifiable people who have done wrong and need to be brought to justice. This implies a threefold restriction on the powers of the state. First, the *people* the state punishes must be limited to evildoers or lawbreakers. Secondly, the *force* used to arrest them must be limited to the minimum necessary to bring them to justice. Thirdly, the *punishment* given must be limited in proportion to the evil which they have done. All three—the people, the force and the punishment—must be carefully controlled.

The same principles have to be applied to soldiers as to the police. Indeed, the distinction between them is a comparatively modern one. The enforcement of law, the maintenance of order, and the protection of the innocent, which today are usually the work of the police, were in Paul's day the responsibility of Roman soldiers. Still in our own times there are situations of civil disorder (e.g. during the Mau Mau rebellion in Kenya and the present communal violence in Northern Ireland) in which the army is called in to supplement the police. Whenever this happens, the behaviour of soldiers has to be understood as an extended form of police action and regulated accordingly. The British Ministry of Defence, for example, explains existing law relating to security operations by the 'useful catchphrase "minimum necessary force" ': 'No more force may be used than is both necessary and reasonable in the circumstances. The degree of force can never be reasonable if it is more than that required to achieve the immediate aim'—the main aims being the prevention of crime and the arrest of criminals.

What, however, if the disturber of the peace is not an individual or group but another nation? The argument now is that, by legitimate extrapolation, the state's God-given authority to administer justice includes the restraint and resistance of evildoers who are aggressors rather than criminals, and so the protection of its citizens' rights when threatened from outside as well as from inside. True, the analogy is not exact. On the one hand, the state which goes to war is acting as judge in its own cause and not as a third party arbitrator, while on the other the cool judicial procedures of the law court have no parallel in the declaration and conduct of war. These differences are due to the fact that acceptable international justice (in arbitration, intervention, and peacekeeping) is only in its infancy. Nevertheless, the development of the 'just war' theory 'represented a systematic attempt to interpret acts of war by analogy with acts of civil government,' and so to see them as belonging to 'the context of the administration of justice' and as subject to 'the restraining standards of executive justice.'[13]

Executive justice, however, whether in relation to crime or civil disorder or international warfare, must always be both *discrimi-nate* action (limiting the people involved to evildoers who have to be brought to justice) and *controlled* action (limiting the force used to the minimum necessary to secure this end).

This brings us to the question whether such a limited justification of the use of force could apply to a war in which nuclear weapons are used (since they appear to be indiscriminate and uncontrolled), and so to the third Christian attitude to war.

(3) Relative (or Nuclear) Pacifism

The invention of nuclear weapons has brought an entirely new dimension to the debate about war. The old categories of conventional wisdom seem as obsolete as the old weapons of conventional warfare. Both scientists and theologians are calling for new and bold thinking. As the Roman Catholic bishops said at the Second Vatican Council, the church has 'to undertake a completely fresh appraisal of war.'[14] For everybody knows that if nuclear war were ever to be unleashed, the casualties would be numbered in hundreds of millions, and could not be limited (as they largely have been in the past, though indeed less this century) to armies confronting one another.

The relevant biblical principle, which we need to evoke and apply, seems to be the great evil of 'shedding innocent blood.' The importance of 'blood' in Scripture is that it is the carrier and so the symbol of life.[15] To 'shed blood' is therefore to take life by violent means, in other words to kill. But human life, being the life of human beings made in the image of God, is sacrosanct. In the Old Testament the shedding of human blood was divinely permitted in virtually one situation only, namely in the execution of a murderer. It is true that in the Mosaic law a small number of other serious offences (e.g. kidnapping, cursing parents, sorcery, bestiality, idolatry, and blasphemy, Exodus 21, 22 and Leviticus 24) were punishable by death. But this does not override the principle: 'whoever sheds the blood of man, by man shall his blood be shed, for in the image of God has God made man' (Genesis 9.6). That is, the bloodshedding of murder deserves the bloodshedding of capital punishment. For in the latter case it is the blood of the guilty which is shed. In all other cases, the sin of 'shedding innocent blood' has been committed.

This understanding was enshrined in the Old Testament provision of six 'Cities of Refuge,' three on each side of the River Jordan, carefully sited to cover the whole country. It was based on the distinction between murder (intentional killing) and manslaughter (unintentional), and was designed to protect the manslayer from the 'avenger of blood' and so avoid the shedding of innocent blood.

A distinction was made in Old Testament times not only between murder and manslaughter, but also between blood shed in war (which was permissible) and blood shed in peace (which was not). Thus when Joab killed both Abner and Amasa, the two commanders of Israel's army, David condemned him for 'avenging in time of peace blood which had been shed in war,' and so bringing upon David's house the guilt of shedding innocent blood (1 Kings 2.5, 31-34, RSV).

Against this background of Old Testament law, the prophets uttered fierce denunciations against Israel. Jeremiah warned them of God's coming judgment because they had forsaken him and profaned Jerusalem. How? They had 'burned sacrifices in it' to other gods and 'filled this place with the blood of the innocent' (19.4). Thus idolatry and bloodshed were bracketed. No sin against God was worse than worshipping idols. No sin against man was worse than shedding innocent blood. Similarly, Ezekiel described Jerusalem as bringing doom upon herself 'by shedding blood in her midst' and 'by making idols' (Ezekiel 22.1-4 cf. 36.18). Both these prophets coupled worshipping idols and killing the innocent as the two paramount sins.

The same horror over the shedding of innocent blood continues in the New Testament. Judas confessed that he had 'betrayed innocent blood' (Matthew 27.4), and when Pilate claimed to be 'innocent of this man's blood,' the people recklessly responded 'Let his blood be on us and on our children' (Matthew 27.24, 25).

The biblical evidence on this matter is an impressively united testimony from the time of the patriarchs through the law and the prophets to the New Testament. Human blood is sacrosanct because it is the life of godlike human beings. To shed the blood of the innocent is therefore the gravest social sin, whether committed personally in murder or judicially by an oppressive regime. The reason God's judgment fell on Israel in the seventh century B.C. is that they were guilty of shedding much innocent blood, and in the first century A.D. because they shed the innocent blood of Jesus Christ. 'Hands that shed innocent blood' are among the things which Yahweh is said to hate (Proverbs 6.16, 17).

This biblical message must not be evaded. The judicial authority God has given the state, including the use of 'the sword' (Romans 13.4), is strictly limited. In the case of the police it is to be used only to arrest criminals and bring them to justice, in the case of the army only to engage in a just war by just means for a just end. In both cases the immunity of the innocent is to be ensured—of law-abiding citizens in peacetime and of noncombatants in wartime. Therefore any unlimited, uncontrolled or indiscriminate use of force is forbidden.

In particular, a distinction has always been recognised in war between combatants and noncombatants, between the army and the civilian population. It is true that the army consists of human beings made in God's image, who may have been conscripted against their will, and who may be entirely innocent of the crimes committed by their government. Nevertheless, if it is legitimate to resist an aggressor nation, it is legitimate to regard its army as its agent in a way that its civilian population is not. This distinction is endorsed both by international law ('the protection of civilian persons in time of war') and by biblical teaching (the prohibition of shedding innocent blood). It applies in two ways.

First, the principle of noncombatant immunity condemns the indiscriminate use of 'conventional' (i.e. non-nuclear) weapons. For example, the Christian conscience rebels against the 'obliteration' or 'saturation' bombing of Hamburg, Cologne, and Berlin in 1942 and 1943, and especially of Dresden in 1945. British and American leaders (notably Churchill and Roosevelt) had previously denounced the Nazi bombings of cities as odious and shocking, and the British government publicly announced that it was no part of its policy to bomb nonmilitary targets, whatever the Nazis might do. But the Allies went back on their word, as they had reserved the right to do if Germany did not observe the same restrictions. Allied bombs on Hamburg in 1943 and on Dresden in 1945 created a 'fire storm' of unimaginable horror. It was reckoned that about 135,000 people died in two days of raids on Dresden in February 1945 (considerably more than the immediate deaths caused by the atomic bombs dropped on both Hiroshima and Nagasaki); they included thousands of refugees who were fleeing before the Russian advance.

I for one am thankful that Bishop George Bell of Chichester had the courage to protest in the House of Lords against this policy. Obliteration bombing 'is not a justifiable act of war,' he said, and 'to justify methods inhumane in themselves by arguments of expediency smacks of the Nazi philosophy that Might is Right.' The report of a Church of England commission *The Church and the Atom* (1948) concurred with his judgment, describing the raids on Dresden as 'inconsistent with the limited end of a just war: it violates the principles of discrimination.'[16]

Secondly, the principle of noncombatant immunity condemns the use of indiscriminate weapons. Consider such 'chemical' weapons as poison gas. Its use in World War I was a breach of the 1907 Hague Convention. The 1925 Geneva Protocol bound its signatories (by now nearly every nation) not to be the first to use it. And in World War II no signatory nation broke this pledge. Stories about 'yellow rain,' however, have led to the widespread belief that Soviet troops have used it in Afghanistan, the Communist forces in Kampuchea and Laos, and the Iraqis in their war with Iran. Modern nerve gases are to the chemist what nuclear weapons are to the physicist. Gas masks would offer no protection, because these gases would penetrate the skin. If dropped from the air, it is reckoned that twenty civilians would be killed to one combatant, because only combatants would be issued with protective clothing.

'Biological' (sometimes called 'bacterial') weapons were also included in the renunciations of the 1925 Geneva Protocol. Each nation-signatory undertook not to be the first to use either gas or germs. The Biological Weapons Convention of 1971 went further and called for the abolition of stockpiles, although no verification procedures were agreed.

The third kind of indiscriminate weapon is 'atomic' or 'nuclear.' These three (Atomic, Biological, and Chemical) are sometimes referred to as 'ABC' weapons; they surely constitute the most gruesome alphabet ever conceived. The invention and refinement of ABC weapons, especially of nuclear devices, have radically changed the context in which to think about the morality of war; they challenge the relevance of the 'just war' theory. A war could still have a just cause and a just goal. But at least if macroweapons were used ('strategic' or 'tactical'), there would be no reasonable prospect of attaining the goal (since nuclear wars are not winnable) and the means would not be just, since nuclear weapons are neither proportionate, nor discriminate, nor controlled. Millions of noncombatants would be killed. In a nuclear holocaust much innocent blood would be shed. Therefore the Christian conscience must declare the use of indiscriminate nuclear weapons, as also of chemical and bacterial weapons, immoral. A nuclear war could never be a just war.

A Christian consensus on this issue seems to be steadily growing. The Second Vatican Council said: 'Any act of war aimed indiscriminately at the destruction of entire cities or of extensive areas along with their population is a crime against God and man himself. It merits unequivocal and unhesitating condemnation.'[17] The British Council of Churches at its November 1980 Assembly passed the following resolution: 'the development and deployment of nuclear weapons has raised new and grave ethical questions for Christians. Because no gain from their use can possibly justify the annihilation they would bring about, and because their effects on present and future generations would be totally indiscriminate as between military and civilians, to make use of the weapons would be directly contrary to the requirements of the so-called 'just war.' The doctrine of deterrence based upon the prospect of mutual assured destruction is increasingly offensive to the Christian conscience.'[18]

Similarly, the authors of *The Church and the Bomb*, subtitled 'nuclear weapons and Christian conscience'—though the unofficial report of a Church of England working party which General Synod did not endorse—have carried many of their readers with them in their theological and moral conclusions: 'We must conclude that the use of nuclear weapons cannot be justified. Such weapons cannot be used without harming noncombatants and could never be proportionate to the just cause and aim of a just war.'[19]

Again, 'It is in our view proven beyond reasonable doubt that the Just War theory . . . rules out the use of nuclear weapons. The damage to non-combatants . . . ; the havoc made of the environment; and the dangers to generations yet unborn; these things make nuclear weapons indiscriminate and nuclear war almost inevitably disproportionate. The evils caused by this method of making war are greater than any conceivable evil which the war is intended to prevent, and they affect people who have nothing to do with the conflict.'[20] Again, 'we shall have failed wholly in our presentation if we have not made it clear that in our view *the cause of right cannot be upheld by fighting a nuclear war.*'[21]

Evangelical Christians have been slow to catch up with the biblical perspectives of other sections of the Church. In 1980, however, an ecumenical group (with strong evangelical participation) met in the United States, saw a parallel between the nineteenth-century movement to abolish slavery and the need for a twentieth-century movement to abolish nuclear weapons, and issued 'The New Abolitionist Covenant.' It includes these sentences: 'Unlimited in their violence, indiscriminate in their victims, uncontrollable in their devastation, nuclear weapons have brought humanity to an historical crossroads. More than at any previous time in history, the alternatives are peace or destruction. In nuclear war there are no winners.'[22]

This Christian consensus is not universal, however. It is important to consider the questions which are being asked about it, and the qualifications which are being suggested.

Questions and Qualifications

First, some are maintaining that *the distinction between combatants and noncombatants is obsolete*. That is, modern war is total war, and there are no noncombatants any longer. The nation's whole population is sucked into the war effort. Every taxpayer is helping to finance it. Even people in civilian jobs are thereby releasing others for military service. Therefore, since everybody is involved, the use of indiscriminate weapons is legitimate.

In reply, we agree that the old clear-cut distinction between a country and its small professional army no longer applies, and that certainly anybody engaged in the manufacture, deployment or use of weapons may be regarded as a combatant. Nevertheless, there are still some categories like elderly people, little children, and the physically and mentally sick, who should be guaranteed noncombatant immunity, for to kill such people would clearly be to shed innocent blood.

It will not do to quote Old Testament examples of universal slaughter, since in such cases we are specifically told that the guilt was universal too. They were, therefore, not 'indiscriminate' judgments. Before the Flood 'the LORD saw how great man's wickedness on the earth had become, and that every inclination of the thoughts of his heart was only evil all the time' (Genesis 6.5). Sodom and Gomorrah would have been spared if only ten righteous people could have been found there (Genesis 18.32), while the Canaanites' practices were so depraved and detestable that the land itself is said to have 'vomited out its inhabitants' (e.g. Leviticus 18.25). Can it be seriously maintained that a similar situation prevails in the Soviet Union, millions of whose peasant people are devout members of the Russian Orthodox Church, while many others are evangelical Protestants? The East is far from being wholly evil, and the West from being wholly good.

If the universal judgments of the Old Testament supply no

precedent for indiscriminate warfare, what about the Old Testament principle of corporate solidarity or responsibility? God described himself as 'punishing the children for the sin of the fathers to the third and fourth generation' of those who hated him (Exodus 20.5), and the humiliated survivors of the destruction of Jerusalem complained: 'Our fathers sinned . . . , and we bear their punishment' (Lamentations 5.7). Does not this divine action, it is asked, justify the slaughter of the innocent with the guilty in war? No. The principle was exemplified in God's dealings with his people as a nation; it was not transferred to the lawcourts, where guilt had to be established. If therefore we are right that a moral defence of the just war is possible only if it can be seen as an extension of the administration of justice, then the distinction between the innocent and the guilty must somehow be preserved.

Secondly, it is pointed out that *not all nuclear weapons are indiscriminate.* During the immediate postwar years and during the Dulles era of the fifties the allied policy was indeed to threaten 'massive retaliation.' President Eisenhower in his 1958 State of the Union message spoke of 'the prospect of virtual annihilation' which awaited the aggressor. But the 1960s brought nuclear stalemate, and in 1962 Defence Secretary Robert McNamara developed the 'counter-force' concept, namely that retaliation would be limited to the destruction of the enemy's military installations, not cities. Today the key expressions are 'flexible response' and 'graduated response,' which (it is claimed) could be contained. Besides, during the last two decades both 'tactical' and 'theatre' (as opposed to intercontinental or 'strategic') weapons have become so sophisticated that they could home in on precise targets with incredible accuracy. And the Enhanced Radiation Weapon or 'neutron bomb' can immobilise a single tank by killing its crew. So, as the processes of miniaturisation and precision targeting continue, nuclear weapons will become increasingly discriminate in their effects, and their use cannot be given a blanket condemnation. That is the argument.

There is plainly some cogency in this reasoning. The less indiscriminate weapons become, the less unacceptable they are. There might conceivably, therefore, be a situation in which it would be morally permissible to use a very limited nuclear weapon, even though there would be some degree of radioactive fallout, and therefore some noncombatants would probably be killed. It would have to be a situation of the utmost urgency, in which the only alternative would be the worse evil of surrender to a godless regime.

But before the Christian conscience could depart from its absolute renunciation of nuclear weapons, it would need to be convinced that the use of a limited weapon would almost certainly be effective and cause the enemy to back off. For the alternative is the grave risk of escalation by the losing side. It is true that not all experts consider escalation inevitable. Michael Quinlan claims that 'escalation is not an inexorable scientific process; it is a matter of human decision.'[23] Yet this is the most hazardous speculation. He admits that we do not know what would happen, because (mercifully) we have had no experience of this situation. I think the American Roman Catholic bishops were wiser in their Pastoral Letter to express their 'extreme scepticism about the prospects for controlling a nuclear exchange, however limited the first use might be.'[24] Similarly, the Public Hearing on Nuclear Weapons and Disarmament, organised in Amsterdam in 1981 by the World Council of Churches, reported: 'the weight of the evidence convinces us that the risks are too great, and that there is no moral justification for believing that a limited nuclear war could remain limited.'[25]

The majority of experts and commentators are predicting that, once the nuclear threshold or 'firebreak' has been passed, escalation could not be halted. The official and public policy of the Soviet Union is certainly to respond to any use of nuclear weapons by NATO with a massive nuclear retaliation. 'What is almost universally agreed,' writes General Sir Hugh Beach, 'is that once a single nuclear weapon has been used by either side, a boundary of almost unimaginable danger will have been crossed. *The Church and the Bomb* is fully justified in drawing attention to the central importance of "escalation." It is a metaphor drawn from the moving staircase and implies that once embarked upon the bottom step you can neither get off nor turn back, nor is there any emergency stop button.'[26]

Three months before he was killed by an IRA bomb, Earl Mountbatten of Burma made an eloquent speech about the horrors of nuclear war. 'A new world war,' he said, 'can hardly fail to involve the all-out use of nuclear weapons.' So, 'in the event of a nuclear war there will be no chances, there will be no survivors—all will be obliterated.'[27]

In the Roman Catholic study *Nuclear Deterrence—Right or Wrong?* Roger Ruston quotes Lord Cameron as agreeing that 'in any battlefield use of nuclear weapons the risk of escalation must be immensely high,' and former Defence Secretary, Harold Brown, as saying that 'what might start as a supposedly controlled, limited strike could well—in my view would very likely—escalate to a full-scale nuclear war.' Roger Ruston's own conclusion is that all uses of nuclear weaponry 'would very probably result in mass slaughter of innocent people.'[28] The Palme Report (1982) is even stronger: 'We on the Commission are firmly of the mind that there would be virtually no likelihood of limiting a nuclear war, once begun.'[29] Again, 'once the nuclear threshold has been crossed, the dynamics of escalation would inexorably propel events towards catastrophe.' Therefore, they urge nations 'to maintain a clear nuclear threshold, . . . a clear distinction between nuclear and conventional weapons' and 'to abstain from deploying weapons which blur the distinction by appearing to be more "useable." '[30]

If the risk of escalation is as great as these quotations indicate, then the only way of safety is to ensure that the nuclear threshold is never crossed.

The third question which people ask nuclear pacifists is this: *If the use of nuclear weapons would be evil, must not their retention as a deterrent be declared equally evil?* Supposing we agree that the use of macronuclear weapons, being agents of indiscriminate destruction, would be immoral, and that the risk of escalation is too great to justify the use of microweapons, does that not mean that all Christians should be committed to unilateral nuclear disarmament? No, not all relative (or nuclear) pacifists are unilateralists. For there is a moral distinction between possession, threat, and use.[31] It is probably true that if an action is immoral, then the active threat to perform it is immoral too. But the possession of nuclear weapons is more a conditional warning than an aggressive threat. Indeed, since the intention behind possession is not to encourage use but to deter it, possession cannot be pronounced as immoral as use.

Shall we then renounce use but defend possession? This seems to be the conclusion to which we are coming. Of course we can immediately see its logical inconsistency. For the effectiveness of a deterrent depends on the skill (technical) and the will (moral and political) to use it if necessary, and on the belief of the enemy that we intend to do so. A deterrent lacks credibility if the enemy knows we would never use it, and if it lacks credibility it loses its power to deter. So 'retaining possession, renouncing use,' though morally defensible, seems practically self-defeating. We are caught between the ineffective and the immoral, or rather between a moral stance which is ineffective and an effective deterrent which (if used) would be immoral, and so between principle and prudence, between what is right and what is realistic. Professor Wolfhart Pannenberg has put his finger on this tension in a recent book. He writes about 'the conflict . . . between two different ethical attitudes: an ethics of conviction that adheres to the purity of moral principles, and an ethics of responsibility that feels obliged to consider the consequences that might follow from the decision embraced.'[32]

Speaking for myself, however, I am not willing to be forced to choose between Christian idealism and Christian realism, if I may use these terms loosely. Nuclear pacifists are certainly idealists, who perceive clearly and refuse to compromise the principle that the use of weapons of indiscriminate destruction would be immoral. But in clinging to this ideal, we must also face the realities of evil in our fallen world and of the current situation which reflects it. How then can we reconcile the ideal and the reality? Is there any escape from the dilemma which I have expressed as 'immoral to use, prudent to keep'?

First, I accept the argument that immediate unilateral disarmament might well make nuclear war more rather than less likely. It might tempt the Soviet Union to exploit our self-imposed weakness. They might either bully us into surrender by using nuclear missiles without fear of retaliation (in which case we have precipitated use by others through forswearing use ourselves) or blackmail us by threatening to use them (in which case our renunciation will have encouraged a Communist take-over). The question is how to prevent the use of nuclear weapons by *both* sides, and at the same time preserve our freedom. It seems to be safer therefore, and more consistent with both ideal and reality, to retain a nuclear deterrent while developing the search for a disarmament which is mutual, progressive, and verifiable.

Secondly, the retention of a deterrent whose weapons it would be immoral to use can be morally justified only as a temporary expedient. As Pope John Paul II said in June 1982 to the UN Second Special Session on Disarmament, the nuclear deterrent 'may still be judged morally acceptable,' but only if it is seen 'certainly not as an end in itself, but as a step on the way towards a progressive disarmament.' This should increase the urgency with which the quest for effective disarmament proposals is pursued.

Thirdly, within the framework of bilateral disarmament there is a place for imaginative unilateral initiatives, which Pope John Paul II has called 'audacious gestures of peace.' True, some have already been taken by the West without being reciprocated (e.g. the American removal from Europe in 1979 of a thousand nuclear warheads). Yet more can surely be taken without undue danger. The West should persevere, and in particular have the courage to declare a 'no first use' commitment.

Fourthly, whether or not our conscience can accept a distinction between limited and unlimited nuclear weapons, we should be able to agree that the latter should be renounced and abolished as soon as possible. Professor Keith Ward, for example, who on the moral principle that we may 'commit an evil act (one causing harm) in order to prevent a much greater evil' thinks that the use of a limited nuclear weapon might in an extreme situation be the lesser of two evils, nevertheless declares that 'all-out nuclear war must . . . stand unequivocally condemned. . . . It is morally unjustifiable.' 'It is therefore imperative,' he adds, 'to dismantle the apparatus which makes all-out war possible,'[33] and to retain only 'a limited nuclear deterrent,' indeed the minimum necessary to deter. Nuclear 'superiority' is entirely unnecessary; nuclear 'sufficiency' is enough. Moreover, because of the enormous 'overkill' of the superpowers' current arsenals, to reduce them substantially would not appear to entail unacceptable risk. And such a reduction *might* be the impetus which is needed to start the downward spiral of disarmament on both sides.

Meanwhile, fifthly, the deterrent must somehow remain credible. If the use of nuclear weapons would be immoral, we cannot encourage NATO to threaten their use. Yet if we want the deterrent to deter, we cannot encourage NATO to bluff either. The only alternative seems to be to cultivate uncertainty. NATO leaders might say to the USSR 'we believe that the use of weapons of indiscriminate destruction would be both crazy and immoral. We are determined not to use them. We are sure you do not want to use them either. Yet if you attack us, you may provoke us to act against both our reason and our conscience. We beg you not to put us in that position.'

This brings us to the fourth question which is addressed to relative (nuclear) pacifists: *Would not a Communist take-over of the West be a greater evil even than nuclear war?*

The scenario which is frequently envisaged and greatly feared, is that the Allies, threatened with defeat by an invading Soviet army equipped with superior conventional weapons, would be tempted in self-defence to resort to nuclear weapons, and so would plunge the world into nuclear war. Would that not be justified? we are asked. Can we seriously envisage the possibility that western countries would allow their territory to be overrun and subjugated? For, if we anticipate the worst that might happen, then the freedoms we have come to accept as indispensable to our quality of life would be brutally suppressed. Churches would be closed and Christians harassed. Atheism would be taught in our schools, and the Christian education of children prohibited. Dissidents would be arrested, and without a fair trial consigned to prison, labour camp or psychiatric hospital. The whole hateful apparatus of the Gulag would be installed. We would find ourselves enslaved. Millions would die. The long dark night of the world would have begun.

Would not such an evil be literally 'intolerable,' worse even than the evil of nuclear war? True, the evil of subjugation would be perpetrated by the atheistic aggressor, not by us. Yet if it could be avoided by some moral action on our part, and we do not take action, we would become accomplices in the evil. If something could be done, then to do nothing is to do evil. On the other hand, if the 'something' which could be done to prevent a take-over is a resort to nuclear war, we are back with the original question: Which is the greater evil?

The ethical dilemma which faces Christians cannot be summed up by either of the two naive maxims 'better dead than red' or 'better red than dead.' The first implies that to live under Communist rule would be the worst possible calamity which could befall human society, and that even a nuclear holocaust would be preferable. The opposite maxim, 'better red than dead,' implies that nuclear death would be so horrible that even life under Communist rule would be preferable. But both these positions are sub-Christian because amoral. The first is defeatist; it ignores the witness of history that the human spirit cannot be crushed by even the most brutal tyranny. The second is materialistic; it rests on the secular assumption that physical suffering and death are the end of everything.

Nuclear pacifists, however, are concerned about moral principle, not prudential balance. Our position is this: To start (or share in starting) a nuclear war would be a moral evil of such magnitude that no situation could ever justify it, not even the fear that we ourselves would otherwise be red or dead or both.

How can we hope to preserve our values by violating them? Would it not be better to live under an oppressive Communist regime, with all the suffering and slavery that would involve, than be responsible for destroying the whole of human civilisation? It would be appalling indeed to allow millions of people to be deprived of liberty; but would we be prepared to incinerate millions in order to prevent it happening? Would it not be better to suffer injustice ourselves than inflict it on others? This is not 'better red than dead'; it is 'better to endure a red régime ourselves, than be the cause of millions of other deaths.'

In the end, then, we have to decide which blessing we value the more: social freedom, though at the cost of losing our moral integrity by starting a nuclear war; or moral integrity as a nation, though at the cost of losing our social freedom by allowing our country to be overrun. If this might one day be the option before us, I hope we should know which to choose. It would be better to suffer physical defeat than moral defeat; better to lose freedom of speech, of assembly, even of religion, than freedom of conscience before God. For in his sight integrity is yet more valuable than liberty.

Christian Peacemaking

Jesus spoke of both war and peace. On the one hand, he warned us of 'wars and rumour of wars'; on the other he included in his characterisation of the citizens of God's Kingdom the active role of peacemaking. He pronounced his peacemaking followers both blessed by God and the children of God (Matthew 5.9), for peacemaking is a divine activity. God has made peace with us and between us through Christ. We cannot claim to be his authentic children unless we engage in peacemaking too.

What practical peacemaking initiatives is it possible for us to take?

(1) Christian Peacemakers Must Recover Their Morale

There are two tendencies in today's Church which undermine Christian morale. Both must be firmly repudiated.

The first is the tendency to trivialise the nuclear horror, or to grow so accustomed to the escalating balance of terror that we lose our sense of outrage. Examples of the ease with which we acquiesce in the prospect of nuclear war were given in April 1982 by Roger Molander, a former White House nuclear strategist for the National Security Council, and now Executive Director of *Ground Zero*, a nuclear war education project. He used, he said, to stick different-coloured pins (representing different-sized weapons) into a map of the Soviet Union. For example, a pink pin for Minsk meant another 200,000 dead. A visitor who watched him was horrified. 'But,' he explained, 'when the pin went into Minsk or Moscow, I didn't see people working or children playing. I assumed that someone above me in the system thought about those things. Me: I just stuck in the pins.'

Roger Molander's second example concerned a Navy captain who, at a meeting in the Pentagon, said people were getting too excited 'as if nuclear war would be the end of the world, when, in fact, only 500 million people would be killed.' Only 500 million people! Within a generation, the Navy captain went on, 'genetic engineering would make people immune to radiation.' 'I reached for my hat,' concluded Roger Molander, 'knowing how Woody Allen felt in "Annie Hall" when he excused himself from a conversation saying that he had "an appointment back on planet Earth." '[34]

Similarly, we need to watch our vocabulary. Robert W. Gardiner has given examples of the 'ingenious rhetoric' we use to reduce the horror of nuclear war. A projectile which destroys millions but deposits little fallout is called 'a clean bomb'; weapons of mass destruction are given 'diminutive and affectionate labels' like 'nukes'; 'Bambi' is the name of a missile (i.e. 'don't be afraid of nuclear missiles, they're really cute, harmless little things'); and as for 'nuclear umbrella,' what could be 'more suggestive of the safe, ordinary world of daily living than an umbrella?'[35] We might add the 'nuclear club,' since a club is normally a place of comfort, privilege, and convivial fellowship, not an association of nations whose common denominator is the possession of lethal weaponry.

The second tendency which undermines morale is to be so pessimistic about the future as to acquiesce in the general mood of helplessness. But both indifference and pessimism are inappropriate in the followers of Jesus. We need to recover our sense of indignation about the accelerating arms race and to resolve to join others in seeking to reverse it. As Dr. David Owen has written in his Introduction to *Common Security*, the Palme Commission Report, 'Governments do respond to popular feeling. They can be influenced, particularly if the pressure is coming from a broadly based public opinion.'[36]

(2) Christian Peacemakers Must Pray

Please do not reject this exhortation as a piece of pietistic irrelevance. For Christian believers it is nothing of the sort. Irrespective of the rationale and the efficacy of praying, we have been commanded to do it. Jesus our Lord specifically told us to pray for our enemies. Paul affirmed that our first duty when we assemble as a worshipping congregation is to pray for our national leaders, so that 'we may live peaceful and quiet lives in all godliness and holiness' (1 Timothy 2.2). Yet today 'often the pastoral prayer in public worship is brief and perfunctory; the petitions are so unimaginative and stale as to border on "vain repetitions"; and the people doze and dream instead of praying.'[37] There is a great need to take seriously the period of intercession in public worship, and to pray for rulers and governments, peace and justice, friends and enemies, freedom and stability, and for deliverance from a nuclear conflagration. The living God hears and answers the sincere prayers of his people.

(3) Christian Peacemakers Must Set an Example as a Community of Peace

God's call to us is not only to 'preach peace' and to 'make peace' but also to embody it. For his purpose, through the work of his Son and his Spirit, is to create a new reconciled society in which no curtains, walls or barriers are tolerated, and in which the divisive influences of race, nationality, rank, and sex have been destroyed. He means his Church to be a sign of his Kingdom, that is, a model of what human community looks like when it comes under his rule of righteousness and peace. An authentic Kingdom community will then challenge the value system of the secular community and offer a viable alternative. We can hardly call the world to peace while the Church falls short of being the reconciled community God intends it to be. If charity begins at home, so does reconciliation. We need to banish all malice, anger, and bitterness from both Church and home, and make them instead communities of love, joy, and peace. The influence for peace of communities of peace is inestimable.

(4) Christian Peacemakers Must Contribute to Confidence Building

There has been a lot of study of the postures of aggression which individuals adopt when they feel threatened; there is need for comparable research into the behaviour of states under threat, that is, into the psychology of national aggression. We need to ask ourselves whether the aggressive behaviour of the Soviet Union, in the buildup of her arsenals, may be due partly to insecurity as well as to imperialism. If so, can anything be done to overcome it?

Some draw attention (and rightly so) to the objective evidence of Soviet expansionist ambitions, which sections of the Peace Movement appear to ignore, much as the Peace Movement of the 1930s ignored the evidence of Fascist intentions. (1) There is the Soviet Union's openly-avowed commitment to the worldwide triumph of Marxism-Leninism. Successive Soviet leaders have pledged themselves to 'the consolidation and flowering of the world socialist system' (Yuri Andropov). (2) Such pledges are but a public confirmation of the so-called 'Brezhnev doctrine,' which led to the brutal interventions in Hungary (1956) and Czechoslovakia (1968), the invasion of Afghanistan (1979) and the suppression of 'Solidarity' in Poland (1981). It has been an ugly series of aggressions. (3) There is the increase of Soviet influence in the Middle East and Africa (e.g. Angola and Ethiopia), often through the agency of Cuban troops and East German military specialists. (4) Although, after World War II, first the United Kingdom and then the USA unilaterally destroyed their stocks of poison gas and dismantled their factories, the Soviet Union has never followed suit and is believed today to have 300,000 tonnes of chemical weapons. (5) In 1968 Defence Secretary Robert McNamara froze American ballistic missiles (both land-based and submarine-launched) at 1,710. They remained at this level until 1980. But the Soviet Union passed this figure in 1970 and by 1978 had 2,428 (well above the Salt I ceiling), and is now rapidly catching up with the total number of strategic warheads possessed by the US. As for armed forces' manpower, the Americans have steadily reduced theirs from a peak of over three and a half millions in 1968 to about two millions in the early eighties (largely because of their withdrawal from Vietnam), while the Soviet Union, which never demobilised after World War II, has steadily built up its forces to well beyond America's 1968 peak.

Can this relentless buildup of Soviet power really be explained, it is asked, as a kind of national paranoia? Some think that it can. They believe that the Soviet Union's chosen road to world dominion is primarily ideological not military, by encouraging revolution not waging war. Her main concern, they add, is for the security of her far-flung borders, with NATO encircling her on the west, and China and Japan on the east. Besides, twice this century Russian territory has been invaded by German armies, and in World War II the Soviet Union lost twenty million of her people. 'History and geography thus combine to yield one of the fundamental imperatives of Soviet military policy. The USSR is determined never again to fight a war on its own territory. . . .'[38] Such an interpretation of Russian behaviour is contemptuously dismissed by former dissident Vladimir Bukovsky, however, who now lives in the United States. 'It is no more,' he writes, 'than a shrewd combination of obvious lies, wrong interpretations and very perfunctory knowledge.'[39]

Whichever explanation is correct, I think we have to agree that each superpower *perceives* the other as a threat, and that we should do anything we can to reduce this confrontation of mutual suspicion and fear. One of the most important sections of the 'Final Act' (1975) of the Helsinki Conference on Security and Cooperation in Europe was the 'Document on Confidence-Building Measures' ('CBMs'), designed to remove the fear of sudden attack. In order to eliminate the causes of tension, build trust, and so contribute to the strengthening of peace and security in the world, the participating states agreed (1) to give each other notice twenty-one days in advance of major military manoeuvres and movements, (2) to exchange observers at such manoeuvres, and (3) to promote exchanges among their military personnel. At the Helsinki follow-up meetings, which were held in Madrid in 1981 and 1982, it was agreed to convene a Conference on Disarmament and Confidence and Security-Building Measures in Europe.

My purposes in mentioning the Helsinki and Madrid meetings is to draw attention not to failures of implementation, but to the valuable concept of 'CBMs.' In any situation in which people feel threatened, the Christian response should be to seek to remove fear and build confidence. And there is no reason why CBMs should be restricted to specifically military matters. They should include cooperation in commerce, industry, culture, and development aid to the Third World. There is also room for Christian initiatives to build confidence in other ways. I understand that the Mennonite Central Committee and the Society of Friends arrange student exchanges with countries of Eastern Europe; this facility could be greatly extended. Christian travel agencies could increase the number of tour groups to the Soviet Union and Eastern Europe, for personal contacts break down caricatures and help people to discover one another as human beings. It is even more important for Christian fellowships to be developed across the iron curtain, so that brothers and sisters in Christ may find one another.

(5) Christian Peacemakers Must Promote Public Debate

The peace movements of the West will contribute to peacemaking only if they succeed in stimulating informed discussion. It is high time for a fresh debate with fresh questions. Are nuclear arsenals a deterrent any longer? Is 'moral possession, immoral use' a viable stance or totally self-contradictory? Are we shut up to the straight choice between nuclear deterrence and unilateralism, or are there 'alternative defence policies'?[40] Would the buildup of 'conventional' armies make it safer for nuclear arsenals to be reduced? Would it ever be justifiable to buy national defence at the cost of millions of civilian lives? Which is the more important in the end: national integrity or national security? Such questions—and many more—need to be raised and debated.

One of the most positive recent contributions to public debate is the publication of *Common Security*, the report of the Palme Commission (which included a distinguished Russian leader, Georgi Arbatov, as well as a Pole). It represents a search for an alternative to both deterrence (which offers a 'very fragile protection' against war) and unilateral action (which the Commission does not recommend). Instead, it argues that security ('freedom from both the fact and the threat of military attack and occupation' . . . 'can be achieved only in common, in co-operation with one another.'[41]

As the Brandt Commission argued for North-South economic cooperation, not on moral grounds but for mutual advantage, so the Palme Commission argues for East-West collective security. The six principles of common security which it develops are: (1) All nations have a legitimate right to security. (2) Military force is not a legitimate instrument for resolving disputes between nations. (3) Restraint is necessary in expressions of national policy (our renunciation of unilateral advantages). (4) Security cannot be attained through military superiority. (5) Reductions and qualitative limitations of armaments are necessary for common security, and (6) 'Linkages' between arms negotiations and political events should be avoided.[42]

In application of these basic principles, the Commission proposes a broad programme for substantial progress towards mutual, verifiable arms limitation and disarmament. Reaffirming Salt II, it then goes beyond it to major reductions leading to essential parity at much lower levels, the establishment of a battle-field–nuclear–weapon–free zone in Europe by removing all battlefield nuclear arms 150 kilometres east and west of the border, the maintenance of a clear nuclear threshold (no blurring of the distinction between conventional and nuclear arms), a chemical-weapon-free zone in Europe, a negotiated treaty banning all nuclear tests, a chemical weapon disarmament treaty, universal adherence to the Non-Proliferation Treaty (with adequate verification leading to improved mutual confidence), strengthening the United Nations security system, regional conferences on security, and the creation of regional zones of peace. Of all these (and many other) recommendations, what has chiefly caught the imagination of the public is the proposal for the denuclearization of Europe—what others have called 'disengagement,' that is, the withdrawal of all troops and ground-based nuclear weapons from Central Europe—and later from the whole continent.

Every Christian is called to be a peacemaker. The Beatitudes are not a set of eight options, so that some may choose to be meek, others to be merciful, and yet others to make peace. Together they are Christ's description of the members of his Kingdom. True, we shall not succeed in establishing utopia on earth, nor will Christ's Kingdom of righteousness and peace become universal within history. Not until Christ comes will swords be beaten into ploughshares and spears into pruninghooks. Yet this fact gives no possible warrant for the proliferation of factories for the manufacture of swords and spears. Does Christ's prediction of famine inhibit us from seeking a more equitable distribution of food? No more can his prediction of wars inhibit our pursuit of peace. God is a peacemaker. Jesus Christ is a peacemaker. So, if we want to be God's children and Christ's disciples we must be peacemakers too.

Chapter Six

Our Human Environment

Environmental studies are a comparatively recent development. Only in 1970 did the British Government create a Department of the Environment with a Secretary of State in charge of it,
whose responsibilities also included housing, transport, and local
government. Words like *ecology, habitat, conservation,* and *pollution*
have not long been part of our everyday vocabulary. The reasons
for the modern concern are not far to seek. They are three, especially in relation to each other.

Reasons for Concern

First, *population growth.* It has been known for centuries that world
population is growing. Only since World War II, however, has
the accelerating growth rate been clearly perceived and the disastrous aftermath of the unchecked population explosion been
predicted. It is said that in the year A.D. 1800 there were about
1,000 million people on earth. By A.D. 1900 this had doubled to
2,000 million, and by 1980 doubled again to 4,000 million,
whereas by A.D. 2000 the expectation is that the world population figure will have passed 6,000 million. Since in the 1980s,
with 4,000 million people, one-fifth of them (800 million) are
destitute, it is being anxiously asked how more than 6,000 million people can possibly be fed twenty years later?

The second cause for concern is *resource depletion.* The so-called

'Club of Rome' in 1972 drew the world's attention to the finite nature of the earth's resources. Until then western leaders had confidently been predicting an annual growth rate of four per cent. Now continuous growth and finite resources were seen to be incompatible. And that was still a year before the first oil price shock.

It was E. F. Schumacher who in 1973 popularised the unpalatable truth in his famous book *Small is Beautiful*, subtitled 'a study of economics as if people mattered.' He wrote of 'the failure to distinguish between income and capital where this distinction matters most. . . , namely the irreplaceable capital which man has not made, but simply found. . . .' His first example of this 'natural capital' was fossil fuels: 'Fossil fuels are not made by men; they cannot be recycled. Once they are gone they are gone for ever.' His other example was 'living nature' (the plankton of the oceans, the green surface of the earth, clean air, etc.), much of which was being destroyed by pollution. 'If we squander our fossil fuels, we threaten civilisation,' he wrote; 'but if we squander the capital represented by living nature around us, we threaten life itself.' The folly of 'the modern industrial system,' he continued, was that it 'consumes the very basis on which it has been erected. To use the language of the economist, it lives on irreplaceable capital, which it cheerfully treats as income.'[1]

The third related problem is *runaway technology*. The modern technological revolution, which Alvin Toffler has called 'The Third Wave' (the agricultural and industrial revolutions being the first two), may well have arrived in time to rescue us from our human predicament. But modern technology, apart from the silicon chip and the microprocessor development to which it has led, is extremely greedy for fuel and in fact created the recent energy crisis. It also sometimes seems like a monster which, if it gets out of control, will destroy its creator. For we are learning how delicate is the balance of nature, and how easily it can be upset.

My understanding is that these three factors, together with questions of food supply, capital investment and pollution, and the complexity of their interactions, led to the controversial forecasting of the early 1970s. Two books—*World Dynamics* by Jay

W. Forrester (1971) and *The Limits to Growth* by Dennis Meadows and others (1972)—both emanating from the Massachusetts Institute of Technology, the second sponsored by 'The Club of Rome,' and both using computers, presented in their different ways a very pessimistic—almost alarming—model of the future world, and demanded 'zero growth' as the only solution.

In 1973, however, an interdisciplinary team at the Science Policy Research Unit of Sussex University, headed by Dr. Christopher Freeman, subjected these two models to searching criticism. The results were published in the February 1973 'special issue' of the journal *Futures*, entitled 'The Limits to Growth Controversy.'[2]

These scholars shared with the MIT researchers the same urgent concern about the world's future, but were critical of their conclusions, believing them to be based on highly debatable assumptions. The MIT case rested (1) on plausible guesses about the future world, rather than on precise facts of the real world (which are not available); (2) on ideological values, which influenced their selection and interpretation of 'relevant'—and their omission of 'irrelevant'—data (according to the Sussex team, limits to growth are likely to be determined more by political and social than by physical considerations); and (3) on an underestimate of the possibilities of continuous technical progress. A forecast made in 1970 would not have been able to take oil or nuclear energy into account; similarly, contemporary forecasts cannot predict with any degree of accuracy the future development of solar energy or nuclear fusion.

This academic controversy notwithstanding, *The Global 2000 Report to the President* was commissioned by President Carter in 1977 and presented to (some say 'disregarded by') President Reagan in 1980. Subtitled 'entering the twenty-first century,' and depending on computer-based statistical projections (on the assumption that present trends continue), it claims to be not speculative but authoritative. It lists the main problems with candour and courage: a world population of over 6,000 millions, five-sixths of whom will live in the developing South; enormous deforestation, with a consequent increase of deserts and decrease of fresh water; the extinction of half a million species of animals and plants; and inconceivable urbanization, with Mexico City a gargantuan megalopolis of thirty million inhabitants.

Have Christians anything to contribute to this anxious debate?

The Biblical Perspective

The biblical approach to the environmental issue is to ask this basic question: To whom does the earth belong? It is deceptively elementary. For how shall we reply? The first answer is straightforward. It is given in Psalms 24.1: 'The earth is the Lord's, and everything in it.' God is its creator, and so by right of creation is also its owner. But this is only a partial answer. Here is Psalms 115.16: 'the highest heavens belong to the Lord; but the earth he has given to man.' So then, the balanced biblical answer to our question is that the earth belongs to both God and man—to God because he made it, to us because he has given it to us. Not, of course, that he has handed it over to us so completely as to retain neither rights nor control over it, but that he has given it to us to rule on his behalf. Our possession of the earth is leasehold, therefore, not freehold. We are only tenants; God himself remains (in the most literal sense) the 'landlord,' the Lord of all the land.

This double truth (that the earth is both his and ours) is spelled out more fully in Genesis 1 and 2. In several verses of Genesis 1 the word 'earth' or 'land' occurs:

Verse 10:	*God called the dry ground 'land.'*
Verses 11, 12:	*Then God said, 'Let the land produce vegetation. . . .' And it was so. The land produced vegetation. . . .*
Verse 24:	*And God said, 'Let the land produce living creatures. . . .' And it was so.*
Verse 26:	*Then God said, 'Let us make man in our image. . . , and let them rule . . . over all the earth.'*
Verse 28:	*God blessed them and said to them, '. . . fill the earth and subdue it.'*

We may legitimately make three affirmations from this biblical material. First, *God gave man dominion over the earth.* We note the two divine resolves of verse 26 'Let us make man in our image' and 'let them have dominion over the earth.' We note also the two divine actions in which his resolves were expressed: 'So God created man in his own image' and 'God . . . said to them . . . "Fill the earth and subdue it" ' (verses 27, 28). Thus from the beginning human beings have been endowed with a double uniqueness: We bear the image of God (consisting of rational, moral, social, and spiritual qualities which make it possible for us to know God) and we wield dominion over the earth and its creatures.

Indeed, our unique dominion over the earth is due to our unique relation to God. God arranged an order, even a hierarchy, of creation. He set man midway between himself as Creator and the rest of the creation, animate and inanimate. In some ways we are one with the rest of nature, being a part of it and having the status of a creature. In other ways we are distinct from nature, being created in God's image and being given dominion. Biologically, we are like the animals. For example, we breathe like them ('a living being' Genesis 1.21, 24 and 2.7), eat like them (verses 29, 30) and reproduce like them ('be fruitful and increase,' verses 22, 28). But we also enjoy a higher level of experience, in which we are unlike the animals and like God: we are able to think, choose, create, love, pray, and exercise dominion. This is our intermediate position between God and nature, between the Creator and the rest of his creation. We combine dependence on God with dominion over the earth. Gerhard von Rad comments: 'Just as powerful earthly kings, to indicate their claim to dominion, erect an image of themselves in the provinces of their empire, where they do not generally appear, so man is placed upon earth in God's image as God's sovereign emblem.'[3]

Generally speaking, man has obeyed God's command to fill the earth and subdue it. At first his progress was slow, as he graduated from food-gathering to farming. He learned to cultivate the soil, to protect cultivated areas from marauding animals, and to use the earth's produce to feed, clothe and house himself and his family. Next, man learned to domesticate animals, and to harness them to his service, in order to make his labour lighter and to bring him pleasure as well. Then he learned the secrets of power which God had locked up inside the created world—in fire, and later in water and steam, in coal, gas, and oil, and now in uranium, the atom and the mighty silicon chip.

In all this, in man's research, discovery and invention, in biology, chemistry, physics, and other spheres, and in all the triumphs of his technology, man has been obeying God and exercising his God-given dominion. There is no question (at least in principle) of man having behaved like Prometheus who stole fire from the gods. In his progressive control of the earth, man has not been invading God's private sphere and wresting power from him, still less imagining that he has stopped up the gaps in which God used to lurk, so that he can now dispense with him. It is foolish to draw these deductions. Man may not have known it, or humbly acknowledged it, but in all his research and resourcefulness, far from usurping God's prerogatives or power, he has been exercising the dominion God gave him. Developing tools and technology, farming the land, digging for minerals, extracting fuels, damming rivers for hydroelectric power, harnessing atomic energy—all are fulfilments of God's primeval command. God has provided in the earth all the resources of food, water, clothing, shelter, energy, and warmth we need, and he has given us dominion over the earth in which these resources have been stored.

Secondly, *our dominion is a cooperative dominion.* In exercising our God-given dominion, we are not *creating* the processes of nature, but cooperating with them. It is clear from Genesis 1 that the earth was made fruitful before man was told to fill and subdue it. It is true that man can make the earth more fruitful. He can clear, plough, irrigate, and enrich the soil. He can put plants under glass to catch more of the sun. He can manage the soil by rotating his crops. He can improve his stock by selective breeding. He can produce hybrid grains with a fantastic yield. He can mechanize his reaping and threshing by using huge combine harvesters. But in all these activities he is merely cooperating with the laws of fruitfulness which God has already established. Moreover, the 'painful toil' man experiences in agriculture, because of God's 'curse' upon the ground (Genesis 3.17), only modifies but does not override his continuing care of the soil under God's 'blessing' (Psalms 65.9ff).

True again, man is controlling and even accelerating things artificially. But it is an *artificial* control of essentially *natural* processes. It is man cooperating with God. It is a recognition that what God gives is 'nature'; whereas what we do with it is 'culture' or 'cultivation.'

True, God has humbled himself to need our cooperation (namely to subdue the earth and till the soil). But we must also humble ourselves to acknowledge that our dominion over nature would be entirely fruitless if God had not made the earth fruitful, and if he did not continue to 'give the increase.'

This combination of nature and culture, of human helplessness and human prowess, of resources and labour, of faith and work, throws light on the recent fashion of declaring that man has now 'come of age' and that (in his newly acquired adulthood) he can dispense with God. The truth is that mankind has come of age technologically. He has developed extraordinary expertise in taming, controlling and using nature. In this respect he is a *lord*, as God meant and told him to be. But he is also a *child* in his ultimate dependence on the fatherly providence of God who gives him sunshine, rain, and fruitful seasons. E. F. Schumacher quotes Tom Dale and Vernon Gill Carter in this respect: 'Man, whether civilised or savage, is a child of nature—he is not the master of nature. He must conform his actions to certain natural laws if he is to maintain his dominance over his environment.'[4]

Thirdly, *our dominion is a delegated, and therefore a responsible, dominion.* That is, the dominion we exercise over the earth does not belong to us by right, but only by favour. The earth 'belongs' to us not because we made or own it, but because its Maker has entrusted its care to us.

This has important consequences. If we think of the earth as a kingdom, then we are not kings ruling our own territory, but viceroys ruling it on the king's behalf, since the king has not abdicated his throne. Or if we think of the earth as a country estate, then we are not the landowners, but the bailiffs who manage and farm it on the owner's behalf. God makes us, in the most literal sense, 'caretakers' of his property.

God's continuing ownership and caring supervision of the earth (indeed of the universe) is asserted many times in Scripture. We have already considered the assertion of Psalms 24.1 that 'the earth is the Lord's.' This includes all living things which inhabit the earth: 'every animal of the forest is mine, and the cattle on a thousand hills. I know every bird in the mountains, and the creatures of the field are mine' (Psalms 50.10, 11). In the Sermon on the Mount Jesus extended the divine dominion further—from the largest to the smallest of creatures. On the one hand, God makes 'his sun' to rise (it belongs to him), and on the other he feeds the birds, and he clothes the lilies and the grass of the field (Matthew 5.45; 6.26, 28, 30). He thus sustains the whole of his creation; in committing it to us, he has not renounced responsibility for it.

This must be the reason why even Canaan, 'the land of Israel,' did not belong to Israel. True, it was 'the promised land' because God had promised to give it to Abraham's descendants, and did in fact do so. Yet individuals owned land only as representatives of their tribe. No one was allowed to transfer land outside the tribe (Numbers 36.5ff), nor to sell it to anyone in perpetuity. Every fifty years, in the Year of Jubilee, all land was to revert to its original owner. God was teaching that the land was still his, that no human being had freehold rights. True, property rights were acknowledged, so that not only theft but also covetousness were forbidden in the law. Nevertheless, the proprietors were to remember two fundamental truths. First, they were only temporary residents: 'The land must not be sold permanently, because the land is mine and you are but aliens and my tenants' (Leviticus 25.23).

Secondly, they must not keep all the produce of the land for themselves but provide for their needy neighbour out of it. As Professor Martin Hengel has put it, 'the right to property was in principle subordinated to the obligation to care for the weaker members of society.'[5] It is interesting that Pope John Paul II has recently summed up the Christian tradition on this matter in similar terms. In his Encyclical on 'Human Work' (1981) he distanced himself from both Marxist 'collectivism' and liberal 'capitalism.' In the latter case, he explained, the question is *how* 'the right to ownership or property is understood.' He continued: 'Christian tradition has never upheld this right as absolute and untouchable. On the contrary, it has always understood this right within the broader context of the right common to all to use the goods of the whole creation: *the right to private property is subordinated to the right to common use,* to the fact that goods are meant for everyone.'[6]

If therefore our dominion over the earth has been delegated to us by God, with a view to our cooperating with him and sharing its produce with others, then we are accountable to him for our stewardship. We have no liberty to do what we like with our natural environment; it is not ours to treat as we please. 'Dominion' is not a synonym for 'destruction.' Since we hold it in trust, we have to manage it responsibly and productively for the sake of both our own and subsequent generations.

The Conservation Debate

Trusteeship includes conservation. The greatest threat to mankind may prove in the end to be not nuclear war but a peace-time peril, namely the spoliation of earth's natural resources by human folly or greed. All life on earth is dependent on the biosphere, the narrow layer of water, soil, and air in which we live. Yet our record in conserving it, especially in this century, is not good.

Vast acres of soil in America, Africa, and Asia, which were once fertile agricultural land, are now through misuse irrevocable deserts or dustbowls. Worldwide deserts have increased by

150 per cent during the past hundred years, so that almost fifty per cent of the earth's land surface is now desert or semi-desert. The resources of coal might last another two thousand years, but natural gas and oil will not last long into the twenty-first century. The disposal of radioactive nuclear waste is causing grave public disquiet. In the 1960s Lake Erie (which in the '50s had yielded seven million pounds of blue pike every year) became so polluted by industrial and domestic poisons that every living creature in it died; its recovery is only now gathering momentum. Many rivers have suffered the same fate as many lakes.

'The most notorious of polluted rivers,' writes Dr. Ron Elsdon, 'is the Rhine,' for 'the *daily* chemical discharge by German industry into the river in 1973' (especially chloride, sulphate, calcium, magnesium, and nitrate) totalled nearly 62,000 tons.[7]

Then there are the oceans. The effect of pesticides on algae and plankton, on which we depend for oxygen, is incalculable. In the United States alone about 142 million tons of smoke and noxious fumes are dumped into the atmosphere annually. Every ten minutes a four-engine jet aircraft emits two and two-third tons of carbon dioxide. As for the squandering of wood pulp for paper manufacture, a single Sunday edition of the *New York Times* consumes 150 acres of forest land. Indeed, I have read that fourteen acres of forest are being destroyed in the world every minute,[8] and Professor Rowland Moss quotes the suggestion that 'if every human being bought a daily newspaper, all the earth's forests would be destroyed within 30 years.'[9] Some of this destruction of the environment undoubtedly happened as a result of human ignorance (e.g. the early dust bowls). Nevertheless, the Church of England's Board for Social Responsibility was not exaggerating when it said that 'despoiling the earth is a blasphemy, and not just an error of judgment, a mistake.'[10] It is a sin against God as well as man.

At the same time, not all Christians have accepted the responsibility which Scripture lays upon us; some have even used the Genesis story to excuse their irresponsibility. Gavin Maxwell, author of books on otters, especially *Ring of Bright Water*, once wrote how he lost two lovely otter cubs he had brought back from Nigeria: 'A Minister of the Church of Scotland, walking along the foreshore with a shotgun, found them at play by the tide's edge and shot them. One was killed outright, the other died of her wounds in the water. The minister expressed regret, but reminded a journalist "The Lord gave man control over the beasts of the field. . . ." '[11] As Professor C. F. D. Moule rightly comments, 'a crime against sense and sensibility cannot be defended by the appeal to mere texts.'[12]

What about these Genesis texts, however? Are we sure that we have interpreted them correctly? Or are the critics of Christianity right that these verses are to blame for contemporary ecological irresponsibility? The American historian Lynn White, for example, of the University of California, Berkeley, has written: 'Christianity . . . not only established a dualism of man and nature, but also insisted that it is God's will that man exploit nature for his proper ends. . . . Christianity bears a huge burden of guilt.'[13]

More outspoken still is Ian L. McHarg. He is a Scot, who spent his childhood between the ugliness of Glasgow and the beauty of the Firth of Clyde, the Western Highlands and Islands. He became a town planner, an ecologist, and the founder and chairman of the Department of Landscape Architecture and Regional Planning at the University of Pennsylvania. In 1969 he wrote that the Genesis story, 'in its insistence upon dominion and subjugation of nature, encourages the most exploitative and destructive instincts in man rather than those that are deferential and creative. Indeed, if one seeks license for those who would increase radioactivity, create canals and harbours with atomic bombs, employ poisons without constraint, or give consent to the bulldozer mentality, there could be no better injunction than this text,' referring to Genesis 1.26, 28. 'When this is understood,' he continues, 'the conquest, the depredations and the despoliation are comprehensible,'[14] for God's affirmation about man's dominion was 'also a declaration of war on nature.' And he concludes with these words: 'dominion and subjugation must be expunged as the biblical injunction of man's relation to nature.'[15]

In his Dunning Trust lectures in 1972/3, Ian McHarg further extended his assault. He traced western man's attitude to the natural world to 'three horrifying lines' in Genesis 1 about the dominion which God gave to man. 'Dominion is a non-negotiating relationship.' 'If you want to find one text of compounded horror which will guarantee that the relationship of man to nature can only be destruction, which will atrophy any creative skill, . . . which will explain all of the destruction and all of the despoliation accomplished by western man for at least these 2,000 years, then you do not have to look any further than this ghastly, calamitous text.'[16]

Dr. McHarg uses very intemperate language to state his case. Some misguided people (for example, Gavin Maxwell's minister) may have tried to defend their irresponsible attitude to nature by an irresponsible use of Genesis 1. But it is absurd to call this text 'horrifying,' 'ghastly,' and 'calamitous,' and then attribute to it two millennia of western man's exploitation of the environment. So let us look at the text again.

It is true that the two Hebrew words used in Genesis 1.26 and 28 are forceful. The verb translated 'have dominion' means to 'tread' or 'trample' on, so that the paraphrase in Psalm 8 is 'you have put all things under his feet' (v.6 RSV). It is often used in the Old Testament of the rule of kings. The other verb 'subdue' was used of subduing enemies in warfare and of bringing people into subjection or bondage as slaves. So man was commanded to rule the creatures of sea, sky, and earth (verse 26) and to enslave the earth, bringing it into subjection (verse 28). Ian McHarg is right, then? No, he is not.

It is an elementary principle of biblical interpretation that one must not establish the meaning of words by their etymology alone, but also and especially by the way they are used in their context. What I have written earlier about this biblical instruction is germane to the interpretation of these texts. We have seen that the dominion God gave to man was delegated, responsible, and cooperative; that it is intended to express the same sustaining care of the environment as its Creator's; and that, far from exploiting the earth and its creatures, man is to use them in such a way as to be accountable to God and to serve others. We have no liberty (as Ian McHarg did in one of his lectures) to set Genesis 1 and 2 in opposition to each other as if Genesis 2 taught 'cultivation' and Genesis 1 'destruction.' On the contrary, the two passages interpret each other. The dominion God gave man is a responsible stewardship which involves the husbanding of the earth's resources. The Creator does not encourage the destruction of what he has made.

Contemporary Awareness

Certainly our generation is beginning to take this responsibility seriously. Scientists are emphasising the delicate balance of nature. God has established in nature almost unbelievable powers of recuperation and regeneration, and in particular a cycle for the renewal of energy (from sun to earth through plants and bacteria, and back again). It is an example of what Barbara Ward called 'the most majestic unity' of our planet. It is due to natural laws which produce 'a dynamic equilibrium of biological forces held in position by checks and balances of a most delicate sort.'[17] 'They are so intricate,' commented Dr. John Klotz, the American conservationist, 'that they could not have developed by chance.'[18] But if we despoil the green surface of the earth, or destroy the plankton of the oceans, we will quickly reach the point of no return in the recycling process. Our immense modern scientific knowledge teaches us 'one thing above all,' wrote Barbara Ward, namely the 'need for extreme caution, a sense of the appalling vastness and complexity of the forces that can be unleashed, and of the eggshell delicacy of the agents that can be upset.'[19]

There have been a number of encouragements in recent years. In Britain, the Clean Air Acts of 1956 and 1968 have delivered London from the lethal fogs of the early 1950s, the 'pea-soupers' which I remember well from my own boyhood. The London smog of 1952 killed four thousand (mostly elderly) people.[20] By contrast, the smog in Tokyo is so bad that roadside oxygen

vending machines have been made available to police and pedes-
trians and in Europe the current preoccupation is with 'acid rain,'
the dangerous acidification of the air by the burning of fossil
fuels.

Then there is the work of the Royal Commission on Pollution,
which has issued eight or nine reports in the last fifteen years,
relating to air pollution, nuclear power, agriculture, and oil in the
sea. Since the United Nations' Conference on the Human Environment in Stockholm in June 1972, commemorated ten years
later by an international symposium in the same city, concern for
'quality of life' has replaced concern for mere survival. And the
'green' movement with its Ecology Parties is keeping environmental issues in the public eye. There have also been numerous
experiments in the recycling of waste. 'Car shredders' re-use all
the metal and plastic of discarded vehicles. Municipal incinera-
tors (e.g. in Germany, Japan, and USA) burn rubbish, without
polluting the air, in order to generate steam for light and heat.
And the meatpacking industry is said by wags to use everything
except the pig's squeal!

Of course there is room for much more innovation. Only one
per cent of the land area of the earth is under cultivation. If only
a cheaper and more efficient way to desalinate salt water could be
invented, the world's deserts could be irrigated and made to
blossom like the rose. The sea, which covers two-thirds of the
planet's surface, has vast riches in terms of fish protein (not to
mention oil, gas, and mineral deposits). Yet we have not learned
to farm the oceans; we are still at the stage of primitive hunters,
and are guilty of over-fishing too. Enormous sums of money
have been invested in the space programme; I am not myself
convinced, however, that we had a clear mandate to land men on
the *moon* before completing our God-given task of filling and
subduing the *earth*.

Have Christians a distinctive contribution to make to the ecological debate? Yes, we believe both that God created the earth,

entrusting its care to man, and that he will one day recreate it, when he makes 'the new heaven and the new earth.' For 'the whole creation has been groaning as in the pains of childbirth right up to the present time.' Its groans are due to its 'bondage to decay' and its consequent 'frustration.' At the end, however, it will come to share in 'the glorious freedom of the children of God.' That is, its bondage will give place to freedom, its decay to glory, and its pain to the joy of a new world being born (Romans 8.19–22). These two doctrines, regarding the beginning and end of history, the Creation and the Consummation, have a profound effect on our perspective. They give us a respect for the earth, indeed for the whole material creation, since God both made and will remake it.

In consequence, we learn to think and act ecologically. We repent of extravagance, pollution, and wanton destruction. We recognise that man finds it easier to subdue the earth than he does to subdue himself. Ronald Higgins' book *The Seventh Enemy* is significant in this respect, for the first six 'enemies' are the population explosion, the food crisis, the scarcity of resources, environmental degradation, nuclear abuse, and scientific technology. The seventh enemy, however, is man himself, his personal blindness and political inertia in the face of today's ecological challenge. That is why the subtitle of Ronald Higgins' book is 'The Human Factor in the Global Crisis.' Man needs a new self-awareness, and fresh vision, a reawakening of his moral and religious capabilities.[21] But is this possible? Yes, Christians are convinced it is. One of the particular merits of Professor Klaus Bockmühl's booklet *Conservation and Lifestyle* is that he goes beyond the 'Christian criteria' for environmental responsibility to the 'Christian motives.' And in his conclusion he presses the challenge home: 'What is sought from Christians is the motivation for selfless service, which once distinguished the Christian heritage. We should be pioneers in the care of mankind. . . . We should show whence the power and perspective for such a contribution come. We are charged to give an example.' We have to 'reawaken the heart of the gospel ethic.'[22]

At the root of the ecological crisis is human greed, what has been called 'economic gain by environmental loss.' Often it is a question of competing commercial interests (though some multinational corporations now have an environmental department). It is only logical that the consumer should pay the cost of production without pollution, whether in increased prices or (through a government subsidy to the manufacturer) in increased taxes. Christians should not grudge this, if it is the cost of responsible, ecological stewardship.

Also, even while the controversy continues over limits to growth, Christians have to bear witness to the self-evident fact that the earth's resources are not infinite. Ten years ago Dr. John Klotz wrote that 'Science cannot find a way of spreading the standard of living of modern western man all over the globe.'[23] Perhaps the silicon chip brings this prospect nearer. But while the vast disparity between wealth and poverty remains, the Christian is bound to have an uneasy conscience. We should strenuously avoid all wastefulness, not only out of solidarity with the poor but also out of respect for the living environment.

Chapter Seven

North-South Economic Inequality

JUST OVER TEN YEARS AGO WE FIRST HEARD ABOUT THE NEED FOR A 'New International Economic Order' (NIEO). The concept was formulated at the meeting of non-aligned countries in Algiers in 1973. Already nearly a decade before that, in 1964, at the first UNCTAD (United Nations Conference on Trade and Development), the representatives of Third World countries formed themselves into the 'Group of 77' (which has now grown to more than a hundred), in order to promote their own economic concerns. In Algiers, however, the call from the Third World for economic justice became more strident, and more specific too in terms of an NIEO or radical restructuring of the world economy in the interests of the developing countries. This demand was doubtless a flexing of Third World muscle immediately after the quadrupling of the price of oil by the OPEC countries. It also expressed the resolve of countries which had recently obtained their *political* independence to gain their *economic* independence as well.

The following year, to the jubilation of many and the chagrin of some, the General Assembly of the United Nations endorsed the call for an NIEO, and published a few months later a 'Charter

of Economic Rights and Duties of States.' It recognised the propriety of NIEO demands, e.g. for more direct aid and better
credit facilities, for the right to regulate (even nationalize) multinational corporations, for the removal of trade barriers to create
more favourable trade terms, and for more adequate representa-
tion in international decision-making structures like the International Monetary Fund. But little progress was made to implement
these proposals. The next two UNCTADs—in Nairobi (1976)
and Manila (1979)—repeated the cry for more credit, aid, trade,
power, and stability of commodity prices, but the Third World
delegates were disappointed that little if anything was achieved
by then. Then in 1980, at the threshold of the third Development
Decade, the Brandt Commission's report burst upon the scene,
under the title *North-South: A Programme for Survival.*

The Brandt Commission Documents

On any showing *North-South* is a remarkable book. Even its critics (to whom I will come later) concede that it was a great
achievement to produce a unanimous report by eighteen distinguished, independent leaders from five continents and from different political backgrounds after two years' work; that it had the
courage to draw the world's attention to the need for radical action on a global scale; and that it presented its challenge with an
unusual combination of reason and passion. In his personal Introduction Herr Willy Brandt, the former West German Chancellor, describes North-South relations as 'the greatest challenge
to mankind for the remainder of this century,' and expresses his
conviction 'that the two decades ahead of us may be fateful for
mankind.'[1]

It is not possible to do justice in two or three paragraphs to a
wide-ranging report of about three hundred pages. I can only
sketch its background, its main proposals, and its supporting arguments. Its setting is a world whose population will grow to
6,000 million by the year 2000, and in which 'nine-tenths of the
increase will take place in the Third World'[2]; in which, although
during the first two Development Decades some real progress

was made in Third World economic growth, public health, life expectancy, and literacy, yet still 800 million people are destitute, meaning that 'almost 40 percent of the people in the South are ... only barely surviving'[3]; in which 'the North including Eastern Europe has a quarter of the world's population and four-fifths of its income,' while 'the South including China has three billion people—three-quarters of the world's population—but living on one-fifth of the world's income,' and 'over 90 percent of the world's manufacturing industry is in the North'[4]; and in which every two seconds a child dies of hunger and disease.[5] It is essential to know these basic statistics; our Christian thinking must be earthed in reality.

Next, the Commission saw its task as relating to 'international development issues.' It is important, therefore, to be aware of its understanding of 'development.' The Report emphasizes that 'the prime objection of development is to lead to self-fulfilment and creative partnership in the use of a nation's productive forces and its full human potential.'[6]

We should have no difficulty in agreeing with this. 'Development' is much more than 'relief' or 'aid.' Relief is still necessary in emergency situations. Aid is also often needed, especially as a 'pump-priming' operation, although it can both demean people (if it is offered in a patronising way) and make them more rather than less dependent. Development, on the other hand, does not increase dependence: it aims to end it. Also, true development is wider than mere economic growth; it includes dimensions of human experience which are of great concern to Christians. This is why the 'Wheaton '83' Conference of the World Evangelical Fellowship preferred 'transformation' to 'development,' for the transformation Christians desire to promote embraces both individuals and communities, and both the material and the spiritual spheres of human life.

The Brandt Commission report made the same emphasis, at least in principle. 'Development is more than the passage from rich to poor, from a traditional rural economy to a sophisticated urban one. It carries with it not only the idea of economic betterment, but also of greater human dignity, security, justice, and equity.'[7] Towards this development goal the Commissioners called for 'bold initiatives,' and for 'profound changes . . . in international economic relations.' Their immediate 'Emergency Programme: 1980–85' was as follows, although I summarize it here in only the barest outline:

1. A large-scale transfer of resources to developing countries.
2. An international energy strategy.
3. A global food programme.
4. A start on some major reforms in the international economic system. These would include the creation of a new 'World Development Fund,' greater Third World participation in existing international economic institutions, the stabilization of exchange rates and commodity prices, greater access to world markets on more favourable terms, and more regulation of transnational corporations.[8]

How did the Commissioners imagine that the nations of the North could be persuaded to share their resources, skills, and power on such a massive scale? They certainly referred to the sense of 'human solidarity and a commitment to international social justice.'[9] But this was not their main thrust. Instead, they wrote, the 'principle of mutuality of interest has been at the centre of our discussions.'[10] That is, 'North and South depend on each other in a single world economy,' and now that they are 'increasingly aware of their interdependence, they need to revitalize the dialogue to achieve specific goals, in a spirit of partnership and mutual interest rather than of inequality and charity.'[11]

Critics have not questioned the evident sincerity of the Commissioners, although they have tended to call the Report 'visionary' and 'romantic,' failing to take sufficient account of human selfishness. Politically, they have deplored the absence of a Russian representative on the Commission (so that the dialogue has been less 'North-South' than 'West-South'). And economically, critics have drawn attention to the Report's emphasis on the distribution of wealth, without a logically prior concern for its creation.

Professor Brian Griffiths in his 1980 London Lectures, published as *Morality and the Market Place*, develops a still more fundamental criticism, which indeed I mentioned in Chapter 4. He is a reluctant critic, because he too is deeply disturbed that 'hundreds of millions of our fellow human beings who like us have been created in the image of God . . . live in conditions of appalling deprivation.'[12] But he does not accept the Report's analysis or remedies, although to be sure he is in favour of reducing protectionism. His main criticism is of the Report's omissions. Why did the Commissioners fall into the trap of generalizing about 'the South' or 'the Third World'? Why did they not probe the embarrassing question why some Third World countries are developing much faster than others? The different pace of development is not due just to the disparity of available natural resources. The reason is deeper than that, for the causes of Third World poverty concern people, Professor Griffiths argues, and their political, economic, and cultural behaviour. The political factors include mismanagement, the expulsion of racial minorities, extravagance, and corruption on the part of governments and their leaders. Then there is the economic system which they choose and operate. But above all there is the cultural factor, that is, the profound effect of a person's cultural background on his motives, thoughts, aspirations, and actions.

As a matter of fact, the Brandt Commission did not altogether ignore the cultural factor. I wonder if Brian Griffiths came across this statement of theirs:

> No matter how enlightened the plans for the economic and social betterment of people's conditions, they will achieve little unless in parallel the battle is fought at the same time in both North and South, to liberate people from outworn ideas, from the grip of narrowly conceived national interests, and from the passions and prejudices inherited from the past. A new international economic order will need men and women with a new mentality and wider

outlook to make it work, and a process of development in which their full capacities flourish.'[13]

Those are good and necessary sentiments, if a bit vague and general. But Brian Griffiths has rightly seized on Willy Brandt's own assertion, on behalf of the Commission: 'We take it for granted that all cultures deserve equal respect, protection and promotion.'[14] 'While all cultures deserve respect,' Professor Griffiths comments, 'they do not all deserve equal protection and promotion.' On the contrary, how can we wish to 'protect and promote' cultures which actively hinder development, for example, by inculcating a spirit of fatalism and apathy? 'If we really wish to understand the origins of poverty in Third World countries,' he goes on, 'I believe we are driven back to an examination of the culture of different countries and to asking basic questions. Why is it that in some societies individual human beings have the views of the physical world, of the importance of work, and the sense of self-discipline which they do? Why is it that in other societies they do not? . . . Personally, I find it impossible to answer these questions satisfactorily in purely economic terms. It is at this point that economic analysis needs a religious dimension. . . . To the extent that any culture contains Judaeo-Christian values, then surely those facets of that culture deserve especial protection and promotion.'[15]

So Brian Griffiths' main criticism of the Brandt Commission's recommendations is that 'they have a decidedly utopian ring about them. They pay scant attention to the spiritual roots of our economic problems. They totally ignore the relationship between economic structures and economic philosophy. . . . Cultures express values which shape institutions and motivate people—some of which . . . promote wealth and justice and liberty, and others of which do not.'[16]

The 1981 London Lectures in Contemporary Christianity, given the year after those by Brian Griffiths, took the form of a symposium published under the title *The Year 2000 AD*. One of the contributions was by Donald Hay of Oxford University and was entitled *North and South: The Economic Debate*.[17] Most of his essay is concerned with the Brandt Commission report. He points out that the Commissioners tried to induce the North to take action (1) by 'arguments from doom' (that otherwise world war, ecological disaster or economic collapse are inevitable) and (2) by 'arguments from mutual economic interests.'

These two sets of arguments he finds neither convincing nor fully Christian. In their place he restates 'the Christian moral argument,' which is not compassion but justice, especially that 'the primary Christian principle to be applied is *justice* in the access to resources,'[18] i.e. to the resources of education, technology, land, and 'a culture based on hope and not despair about the possibilities for economic development.'[19] By contrast, the North has 'used its power to determine North-South economic relations to its own advantage.'[20]

The publication of the Brandt Commission report, in spite of the criticisms, brought high hopes that at last some action would be taken to redress the North-South economic imbalance. The Commission made the specific proposal that the process should be started by 'a limited summit of heads of governments from the North and the South, and hopefully including the East and China.'[21] As a direct result of this suggestion the summit meeting of twenty-two leaders took place at Cancun, Mexico, in October 1981. Unfortunately, however, it proved to be too large (each leader brought an entourage) and too inflexible (half of its two days was taken up with prepared speeches). Also, before it assembled, President Reagan made a preemptive speech, emphasizing 'the magic of the market place' rather than development aid as the solution to the Third World's problems, and declaring the summit to be entirely informal, with no intention of decisions or resolutions. The outcome has been minimal. The nations of the North appear to be preoccupied with their own economic problems.

So in 1983 the Brandt Commission issued its second document, a memorandum entitled *Common Crisis*.[22] In his Introduction Herr Willy Brandt is even more impassioned than before. Three years have elapsed since the publication of *North-South*, he writes. Meanwhile, some of the Commissioners' worst fears have been confirmed. The prospects for economic recovery have deteriorated rapidly. Further decline could 'cause the disintegration of societies and create conditions of anarchy in many parts of the world.' The Cancun summit fell far short of the Commission's expectations. There are no signs of global cooperation. So Willy Brandt and his colleagues have felt it necessary 'to present an urgent and up-to-date version of our original Emergency Programme,'[23] in the hope of breaking the deadlock and averting economic collapse.

The Commissioners summarize their proposals under five headings:

1. Finance—making more money available to promote recovery.
2. Trade—increasing world trade by resisting protectionist pressures.
3. Food—raising food and agricultural production, to make nations more self-sufficient.
4. Energy—creating a new energy agency to increase energy production.
5. Negotiation—improving the negotiating process between North and South.

I do not think Brandt II contains any proposals of substance which were not in Brandt I. It is the same medicine, though perhaps the mixture is stronger, and certainly the tone of the doctors' appeal is more urgent.

Not being an economist, I lack the expertise to comment either on what shape a 'New International Economic Order' should take or on the specific proposals of the two Brandt Commission documents (the 1980 Report and the 1983 Memorandum). What I do feel able to do, however, is to support the concept of global economic cooperation and to offer some biblical thoughts as justification for continuing to seek it. It is another case of struggling to clarify the principles involved, while leaving the framing of policies to those who have the necessary training, knowledge, and influence. It seems to me that two fundamental biblical principles are involved.

The Principle of Unity

The first is the principle of unity, namely that the planet earth is one, and that the human race is also one. Some claim that it was Buckminster Fuller, the famous inventor of the geodesic dome, who first coined the term 'Spaceship Earth.' Others attribute the first use of the expression to Ambassador Adlai Stevenson. It is certainly true that, during the last speech he made before the Economic and Social Council in Geneva on 9 July 1965, he referred to the earth as a little spaceship on which we are all travelling together, 'dependent on its vulnerable supplies of air and soil.'

The following year Barbara Ward the economist took up the theme in her book *Spaceship Earth*, and a few years later elaborated it with René Dubos in *Only One Earth*.[24] Published in preparation for the 1972 United Nations Conference on the Human Environment in Stockholm, and subtitled 'the care and maintenance of a small planet,' the book is addressed to the question how the growing human population can husband the planet's limited resources for the common good and neither exploit, nor waste, nor destroy them. The last chapter 'Strategies for Survival' ends on a rueful note. Governments have paid lip service to the notion of planetary interdependence by setting up a whole variety of United Nations agencies to develop worldwide strategies. But these international institutions 'are not backed by any sense of planetary community and commitment. . . . The planet is not yet a centre of rational loyalty for all mankind.' Yet such a shift of loyalty is possible, and could well be awakened within us by 'a profound and deepening sense of our shared and interdependent biosphere.' After all, the human race has continually enlarged its allegiance—'from family to clan, from clan to nation, from nation to federation.' So why should it not take the final, logical step? 'Today, in human society, we can perhaps hope to survive in all our prized diversity, provided we can achieve an ultimate loyalty to our single, beautiful and vulnerable Planet Earth.'[25]

This is a clear biblical vision. 'The earth is the Lord's and everything in it, the world, and all who live in it' (Psalms 24.1). I have already quoted this verse in reference to the environment: The earth belongs to God. Now we take note that those who live in it belong to him too, for God has created a single people (the human race) and placed us in a single habitat (the planet earth). We are one people inhabiting one planet. Moreover, these two unities (planet and people) are closely related to one another. For God said 'Be fruitful and increase in number; fill the earth and subdue it' (Genesis 1.28). Thus the one people were to populate and tame the one earth, in order to harness its resources to their service. At the beginning there was no hint of the partitioning of the earth or of rivalry between nations. No, the whole earth was to be developed by the whole people for the common good. All were to share in its God-given riches. This principle of 'distributive justice' still applies today.

But this divine purpose has been frustrated by the rise of competitive nations who have carved up the earth's surface and now jealously guard its mineral deposits and fossil fuels for themselves. Of course the Bible (realistic book that it is) recognizes the existence of nations, indicates that their developing histories and territorial frontiers are ultimately under God's sovereign control, welcomes the cultural diversity (though not all the cultural practices) they have created, and warns us that 'nation will rise against nation' to the end. But it does not acquiesce in this international rivalry. On the contrary, it tells us that the multiplicity of mutually hostile nations with mutually incomprehensible languages is a consequence of God's judgment on man's disobedience and pride (Genesis 11).

The Bible also indicates that one of God's major purposes in redemption will be to overcome the enmity which separates nations and to reunite the human race in Christ. So, immediately after the Tower of Babel episode, God promised through Abraham's posterity to bless all the peoples of the earth (Genesis 12.1–3); he predicted through the prophets that all nations would one day 'flow' like rivers to Jerusalem (e.g. Isaiah 2.2); the risen Jesus told his followers to go and make disciples of all the nations (Matthew 28.19); the Holy Spirit came upon 'all flesh,' the nineteen national groups Luke mentions representing the known world (Acts 2.5–11, 17); Paul describes the accomplishment of Christ's cross in terms both of the abolition of the dividing wall of hostility between Jew and Gentile and of the creation out of the two of 'one new man' or a single new humanity (Ephesians 2.14, 15); and the vision of the redeemed before God's throne is of a countless multitude 'from every nation, tribe, people and language' (Revelation 7.9). It would be impossible to miss this strand of internationalism which appears right through the biblical revelation.

So then, we cannot evade our responsibility to the world's poor people on the ground that they belong to other nations and are no concern of ours. The English tend to exhibit a particularly unpleasant kind of national pride. When we travel on the European Continent, we express surprise that other people do not talk our language, and even annoyance that they expect us to learn theirs. We also have an obnoxious habit of dismissing foreigners with contemptuous epithets. It is enough to call somebody a 'wog,' 'hun,' 'dago,' 'frog,' 'chink' or 'yank'; this puts him beyond the pale of our respect. It should go without saying, however, that Christians should have repented of such conceited attitudes, for there is only one world, and both they and we are citizens of it. The main point of the Parable of the Good Samaritan is its racial twist. It is not just that neighbour-love ignores racial and national barriers, but that in Jesus' story a Samaritan did for a Jew what no Jew would ever have dreamed of doing for a Samaritan.

'Patriotism' is good and right. It is a legitimate love for the fatherland to which in God's providence we belong. But Sir Alfred Duff Cooper was grievously wrong when he remarked (I think in the early '50s) that 'the love of one's country should be like all true love—blind, prejudiced and passionate.' I hope he had his tongue in his cheek, for what he was describing is not 'patriotism' but 'nationalism,' namely a blind and exaggerated loyalty to 'my country right or wrong.' It is nationalism, not patriotism, which leads to framing trade policies which benefit one's own nation at the expense of developing nations. Nationalism is incompatible with the perspective of the Bible and the mind of Christ. Every Christian should seek to become a more committed internationalist, by reading about other countries, visiting them if possible, welcoming overseas visitors into our homes, learning a second language, and making friends with people of other cultures. These things will enrich our own lives. They will also symbolize our resolve to affirm the biblical principle of unity (one planet, one people), to develop a global perspective, and to recognize everybody's unavoidable interdependence.

Is this a starry-eyed concept? Perhaps Christians can by God's grace become internationalists, since the biblical vision of human unity is very clear. But can we expect this of people who do not profess faith in Jesus Christ? Are not elected governments obliged to consider the national interest first? Otherwise they will not be reelected.

In his useful introduction to the problems of international aid and trade, *Trade, Justice and the Wealth of Nations*, Duncan Munro points out that the expression 'the family of nations,' though helpful, is misleading, since 'there is a harmony of interests in family life, which nations cannot share. . . . The family, with its close knit bond between members, . . . is capable of considerable self-sacrifice. . . . The nation, however, is incapable of love.' International relationships have to be based on justice instead. 'But,' he continues, 'the moral philosophers are right in saying that there is no logical necessity for men to choose to act justly on the basis of nature alone.' Only the Christian gospel can supply the necessary motivation.[26]

Duncan Munro is justified in drawing our attention to the differences between the nuclear (or extended) family and the family of nations. Yet we must not acquiesce too readily in the distinction. People do recognise that they belong to the worldwide human family. And there is in all human beings, even since the fall, a basic sense of compassion and justice which can influence their individual and collective behaviour. There is certainly a very widespread concern in the West to help the developing nations and to eradicate poverty. Let me quote Barbara Ward again, this time from her book *Progress for a Small Planet.* She saw the contemporary world as living in an 'unsteady interregnum between imperial ages which may be dying and a planetary society which struggles to be born.' The 'chief new insight of our century,' she claimed, is the 'inescapable physical interdependence' of all human beings.[27] Can this lead to a real cooperation for survival? She commends the theory of 'a global compact based upon the application to the planetary community of certain of the basic principles which govern and harmonize domestic society,'[28] namely the redistribution of wealth by taxation, not charity. Could we not apply this domestic model to the planet?

The first step would be a commitment of the rich nations to giving 0.7 per cent of their GNP to the Third World, rising to 1 per cent, together with indirect taxation of international travel. Yet only the Netherlands nearly succeeded in attaining this goal in 1980, with 'Official Development Assistance' (ODA) at .99 percent. Other developed countries are lagging behind, and some have actually reduced their ODA in the last decade. Thus Britain's ODA decreased from .36 per cent in 1970 to .34 per cent in 1980, while the United States' ODA dropped in the same period from .31 per cent to .27 per cent.[29] We are ready to pay taxes in our own country, Barbara Ward argues, because we are *one nation*; should we not be willing to pay an international tax because we are *one world?*

The Principle of Equality

I move now from the first biblical principle (unity) to the second (equality). Consider the following teaching of the apostle Paul:

> *I am not commanding you, but I want to test the sincerity of your love by comparing it with the earnestness of others. For you know*

the grace of our Lord Jesus Christ, that though he was rich, yet for your sakes he became poor, so that you through his poverty might become rich.

And here is my advice about what is best for you in this matter: last year you were the first not only to give but also to have the desire to do so. Now finish the work, so that your eager willingness to do it may be matched by your completion of it, according to your means. For if the willingness is there, the gift is acceptable according to what one has, not according to what he does not have.

Our desire is not that others might be relieved while you are hard pressed, but that there might be equality. *At the present time your plenty will supply what they need, so that in turn their plenty will supply what you need.* Then there will be equality, *as it is written: 'He that gathered much did not have too much, and he that gathered little did not have too little.'*

2 *Corinthians* 8.8–15

The two references to the goal of equality have been italicized in the text so that we do not overlook them. Yet we need to see them in the whole context of Paul's instruction about the collection for the poor Judaean Christians which he was organising in the Greek churches. He begins by assuring them that his teaching is not a command but a test; he is seeking evidence of the genuineness of their love (v.8). So their giving is to be voluntary. Not in the sense that it is optional (because they are under obligation to share with their more needy Christian brothers and sisters), but in the sense that it is spontaneous and free (an expression of their love for the poor, rather than mere obedience to the apostle).

That leads Paul straight to Christ, and to a sublime statement of his spontaneous grace (v.9). He grounds his mundane appeal for the disadvantaged on the theology of the Incarnation, and the gracious renunciation which it entailed. He makes two references to wealth, and two to poverty. Christ had been rich, but he became poor; not as a meaningless gesture of asceticism, but 'for your sakes,' namely that through his poverty you might become rich. That is to say, because of *our* poverty he renounced his riches, so that through *his* poverty we might share them. It was a renunciation with a view to a certain equalisation. Moreover, both his concern to end our poverty and his decision to renounce his riches were expressions of his 'grace' (v.9), as similar action on our part will be of our 'love' (v.8). For grace is spontaneous, undeserved love.

To his exhortation to prove their love Paul adds some practical advice as to how to do so. They should now complete what a year previously they had desired and begun to do, for desiring and doing must go together, according to their means (vv.10-12). Christian giving is proportionate giving, and is acceptable according to what one has, provided that the willingness is there. Paul is not wanting them to relieve the needs of others by putting themselves in want, for that would be merely to reverse the situation, solving one problem by creating another. No, his desire is rather 'that there might be equality' (v.13). He puts the affluence of some alongside the want of others, and then calls for an adjustment, that is, an easing of want by affluence (v.14). Twice he says this is with a view to *isotēs*, which normally means 'equality,' but can also mean 'fairness' or 'justice.' Finally (v.15), he appeals to an Old Testament quotation about manna. God provided enough for everybody. Larger families gathered a lot, but not too much, for they had nothing over; smaller families gathered only a little, but not too little, for they had no lack. Each family had enough, because they collected according to need, not greed.

Let me try to sum up these instructions, in the reverse order, applying them to the world situation today. (1) God has provided enough for everybody's need (adequate resources in sun and rain, earth, air, and water); (2) any great disparity between affluence and want, wealth and poverty, is unacceptable to him; (3) when a situation of serious disparity arises, it ought to be corrected by an adjustment in order to secure 'equality' or 'justice'; (4) the Christian motive for desiring such 'justice' is 'grace,' loving generosity, as in the case of Jesus Christ who, though rich, became poor, so that through his poverty we might become rich; (5) we are to follow his example in this, and so prove the genuineness of our love. Just *how* a worldwide equalisation could or should be effected is another question. Economists differ. A massive transfer of aid is not necessarily the long-term solution. Whatever the method, however, the motivation for seeking equality or fairness is love.

It may be objected by some that Paul's instructions related to an equalisation within the household of God, Gentile Christians from Greece coming to the aid of Jewish Christians in Judea, and that we have no liberty to extend its application from the church to the world. But I cannot accept this limitation. The 'poor' for whose sake the rich Christ impoverished himself were unbelieving sinners like us. Besides, the principle that grave disparity should be evened out sounds like a universal truth. When Paul wrote 'as we have opportunity, let us do good to all people, especially to those who belong to the family of believers' (Galatians 6.10), the purpose of his 'especially' was not to exclude unbelievers, but to remind us that our first responsibility is to our Christian brothers and sisters. We are still under obligation to 'do good to all people' in whatever way we can.

I need now to interpret Paul's teaching with an important qualification: the 'equality' he sets before us as a goal is relative rather than absolute. He is not recommending a total 'egalitarianism,' by which all people become precisely the same, receiving an identical income, living in an identical home with identical furniture, wearing identical clothes and developing an identical lifestyle. The living God is not the Lord of drab uniformity but of colourful diversity. True, he made us equal in dignity and worth (for we all share his life and bear his likeness). True also, he gives the blessings of sunshine and rain to all humankind indiscriminately (Matthew 5.45). But he has not made us equal in ability. On the contrary, by creation we differ from one another—intellectually (we have different IQs), psychologically (our temperaments vary), and physically (some are handsome, others plain, some are strong, others weak). And the new creation extends this disparity. Although we are 'all one in Christ Jesus' (Galatians 3.28), equally God's children, justified by his grace through faith,

and although we have all received the same Holy Spirit to in-
dwell us, yet Christ by his Spirit bestows on us different spiritual
gifts, whose value differs according to the degree to which they
build up the church.[30]

Personal and Economic Deductions

How then can we put together what we find in the Bible—this
unity and diversity, this equality and inequality? Two answers
may be given. First, there is the question of *personal economic life-
style*. Is there any criterion by which to decide at what level we
should choose to live and how much difference we should permit
between ourselves and others in our neighbourhood? It is a
question which all missionaries have to face, especially when
they go from an affluent situation to a developing country.

The Willowbank Report was helpful on this topic: 'We do not
believe that we should "go native," principally because a
foreigner's attempt to do this may not be seen as authentic but as
play-acting. But neither do we think there should be a conspicu-
ous disparity between our life-style and that of the people
around us. In between these extremes, we see the possibility of
developing a standard of living which expresses the kind of love
which cares and shares, and which finds it natural to exchange
hospitality with others on a basis of reciprocity, without embarrassment.'[31] This strikes me as a very practical rule of thumb.
The moment I am embarrassed either to visit somebody in his
home or to invite him into mine, because of the disparity between our life-styles, something is wrong. The inequality has
broken the fellowship. There needs to be an equalisation in one
or other direction, or both. President Nyerere applied this challenge to the building of a Tanzanian state in which 'no man is
ashamed of his poverty in the light of another's affluence, and no
man has to be ashamed of his affluence in the light of another's
poverty.'[32]

Secondly, this principle can help us in our thinking about
North-South economic inequality. Since we all have equal worth (despite unequal capacity), it must be right to secure equal opportu-

nity for each person to develop his or her God-given potential for the common good. We cannot abolish all inequalities, nor even (because of the diversity of creation) attempt to. It is inequality of privilege we should seek to abolish, in order to create equality of opportunity, for millions of people are unable to develop their human potential. This Christians see to be the real scandal. It is not only an offence to human beings, since they are frustrated and unfulfilled, but also to their Creator who bestowed his gifts on them to be developed and used in service, not to be wasted. Let me comment briefly on equality of opportunity in education, responsibility, and trade.

Education must surely come first. According to the United Nations, 'there are still 34 countries . . . where over 80 percent of the population are illiterate.'[33] We should therefore support every programme which seeks equality of educational opportunity. Universal education is probably the shortest route to social justice, for it develops people's social awareness, and thus gives them the understanding and the courage to take hold of their own destiny. This is the process of 'conscientization,' an ugly word popularised by Paolo Freire of Brazil.

Secondly, the developing nations should be given equality in international responsibility. The International Monetary Fund, the World Bank, and the General Agreement on Trade and Tarriffs were all set up as a result of the Bretton Woods conference in 1944, more than twenty years before the first meeting of UNCTAD at which for the first time representatives of Third World countries had a forum of their own. It would seem to be elementary justice (and the Brandt Report argues for it) that developing countries should be given a greater say in these international institutions which control so much of their economic life. Those affected by decisions made should have a share in the decision-making.

Thirdly, I come to the controversial area of international trade. Many are nowadays calling for 'trade not aid.' They are understandably disillusioned that much aid has either financed the wrong things (e.g. prestigious buildings instead of genuine development which creates jobs, increases exports and helps the poor) or been squandered by incompetence or corruption. And they are further frustrated because it is usually thought unacceptable to lay down conditions for the giving of aid. Yet Brandt I and II continue to call for a massive transfer of resources, and it seems to me the duty of givers or lenders (not least because, in the case of a government or bank, it is not their money which is being transferred) to ensure that it is used for the development purposes for which it is given.

President Nyerere has called for equal access to world markets in place of the developing nations' obligation to 'sell cheap and buy dear.' And again Brandt pleads for less protectionism and more favourable trade terms. Indeed, in principle it is widely acknowledged that justice demands this. It is also recognised, however, that genuine equality in trade is hard to achieve, since the developing nations come to the negotiating table and the marketplace as unequal partners, with unequal bargaining powers. This is partly because (before industrialisation) the products they have to offer are limited by their geography, and partly because they lack the resources (the capital, technology, and skill) to be able to diversify their exports. Probably two-thirds of the world come to the international markets disadvantaged in these and other ways.

It is perhaps equality of opportunity in these three areas (education, responsible decision-making, and trade) which would ensure, more than anything else, a fairer distribution of the world's wealth.

The present situation of North-South inequality ('a gap so wide that at the extremes people seem to live in different worlds'[34]) is not God's fault (for he has provided resources in earth and sea), nor is it the fault of the poor (since they were mostly born into it, though some government leaders are to blame for corruption and incompetence), nor is it necessarily our fault (although our colonial forefathers may have had a share in creating it). We become personally culpable only if we acquiesce in its continuance. In Jesus' story of the Rich Man and Lazarus there is no hint that the rich man was responsible for the poor man's plight. The rich man was guilty, however, because he ignored the beggar at his gate, did nothing about his destitution, failed to use his affluence to relieve the poor man's need, and acquiesced in a situation of gross economic inequality which had dehumanised Lazarus and which he could have remedied. The pariah dogs who licked the poor man's wounds showed more compassion towards him than the rich man. Dives went to hell not because he had exploited Lazarus, but because of his scandalous indifference and apathy.

Our temptation is to use the complexity of macroeconomics as an excuse to do nothing. We need to pray that God will call more of his people to develop new international economic policies, work for political solutions, and give their lives in the field of Third World development, practical philanthropy, and evangelism. But these are the callings of only some.

All of us, however, can feel what Jesus felt—the pangs of the hungry, the alienation of the poor, the indignities of the 'wretched of the earth.' Ultimately, the inequalities between North and South are neither political nor economic but moral problems. Until we feel moral indignation over worldwide social injustice, and compassion for worldwide human suffering, we are not likely to act. What action can we take? We can begin by informing ourselves. As Lazarus lay at Dives' gate, so the Third World lies at ours. Dives could not plead ignorance; nor can we. We should ensure that our daily paper has adequate Third World coverage, and perhaps subscribe to a magazine devoted to Third World needs. We could make friends with somebody from a developing country and perhaps offer for short-term service in a Third World situation. Self-education of this kind may lead to political agitation. It will also undoubtedly affect our pocket. Those who read this book will all be comparatively rich; they could not afford to buy it otherwise. We should be thankful for the good things God has given us, but also remember the biblical principles of unity and equality. Then we shall give generously to both world development and world evangelization. Our personal commitment to a simpler life-style will not of course solve the world's economic problems. But it will be an important symbol of our Christian obedience and of our share in the grace of Jesus Christ which induced him to empty himself and take the form of a servant.

Chapter Eight

Human Rights

'WHOEVER WISHES TO LIVE A QUIET LIFE,' LEON TROTSKY IS SAID TO have remarked, 'should not have been born in the twentieth century.' In this at least he was right.

Human Rights Violations

This century has been characterised both by violence and by violations of human rights.[1] In the two World Wars approximately sixty million people were killed. Six million Jews were exterminated in the 'holocaust' of Hitler's concentration camps and gas chambers. Millions of dissidents were also liquidated by Stalin in his Siberian labour camps. According to Solzhenitsyn sixty-five million Russians have been killed by their own leaders since 1923. And although the Soviet Union's new Constitution (which was introduced by Brezhnev in 1977 to replace Stalin's) promised liberties, it failed to give those liberties and effectively silences all dissent, so that today in the Soviet Union there are ten thousand named people in prison for their religious beliefs. Idi Amin's reign of terror from 1971–9 cost the lives of between half and three quarters of a million Ugandans. The ruthless killings of the Khmer Rouge between 1975 and 1979 constituted nothing less than genocide; for three million Kampucheans—almost half the country's population—died by execution, disease or starvation.

Latin America remains a continent of widespread repression

and revolution. In Argentina about thirty thousand people have disappeared since 1976, in addition to the thousands who are known to have been killed or exiled. By 1976 Uruguay had the highest known ratio of political prisoners to population: One out of every five hundred citizens is believed to have been arrested or imprisoned.

In Chile the case of Charles Horman has shocked everybody who has read the book or seen the film. He was one of two Americans (whose attachment to Chile's socialist experiment seems to have been more sentimental than ideological) who disappeared during the right wing coup led by General Pinochet which toppled Salvador Allende's Marxist regime in 1973. Ed Horman, the father, sued the State Department officers from Henry Kissinger down to the Santiago Embassy officials for complicity in his son's death, and withdrew the suit only in 1981 while the government was still stonewalling in the name of 'national security.' His attorney, Thomas Hauser, published *The Execution of Charles Horman*, subtitled 'An American Sacrifice,' which implicated the US Administration and drew an immediate three-page rebuttal from the State Department.

Then Costa-Gavras, the Greek-born film director, who had made 'Z' (the documentary about the regime of the Greek Colonels), interviewed the Hormans and Hauser, researched among Chilean exiles, and shot the moving film *Missing* in Mexico City during 1981. In it we watch Ed Horman, an honest Christian scientist, searching for his missing son in the streets, the stadium, the hospitals, and finally, the morgue. But the evident hypocrisy of American Embassy officials changes him from incredulity through disillusion and cynicism to the final conviction that the US was involved not only in his son's 'execution' but in the coup itself. The film ends with the factual statement that Charles' body, though its return to the States was promised at once, was not in fact sent back until months later, by which time no post mortem could establish the cause of his death.

In South Africa the apparatus of apartheid forcibly segregates blacks in the 'Homelands' arbitrarily designated for them. And in addition to this inhuman government policy, by 1979 163 people had died while in police custody, mostly in mysterious circumstances, of whom the best known was Steve Biko in 1977, the leader of the 'Black Consciousness' movement.

In such a list of atrocities we run the risk of selective indignation, as if human rights violations are being perpetrated only by those wicked Russians, those South African racists, or those Latin American oligarchies or military juntas (sometimes, it is claimed, with North American collusion). We British need, therefore, to remember with shame that in 1978 the European Court of Human Rights in Strasbourg ruled that the interrogation methods used briefly in 1971 on 14 IRA terrorist suspects by the Royal Ulster Constabulary violated Article 3 of the European Convention on Human Rights. Although the Court cleared Britain of Irish government charges that these techniques amounted to 'torture,' it nevertheless described them as 'inhuman and degrading treatment.' The British government accepted the Court's ruling, set up a review committee, and implemented the committee's recommendations.

There are many other ways in which human beings are being oppressed. The United Nations Commission on Human Rights receives about twenty thousand complaints every year. There has been, and in some cases still is, the unjust treatment of minorities, for example, of Asians in East Africa, Indians in Brazil, aboriginals in Australia, untouchables in India, Kurds in Turkey, Iran, and Iraq, Palestinians in the Middle East, Indians in North America, 'Inuit' (Eskimos) in Canada, and perhaps one should add Roman Catholics in Northern Ireland. There is the plight of refugees, and the human degradation caused by illiteracy, racism, poverty, hunger, and disease. And there is the new problem in the West created by the invasion of privacy and the storage of information by computer banks. Worse than all these, however, is the continuing use of torture, in spite of its universal condemnation. Dr. Emilio Castro has written correctly: 'Torture kills the human in the torturer and crushes the personality of the one tortured.'[2]

Concern for Human Rights

Alongside the violation of human rights, even while abuses and outrages have increased, there seems to have been a corresponding growth in the recognition of rights and in concern for their safeguarding. In a sense this is not new. Being a self-conscious being, man has doubtless thought about himself and his identity, his duties and his rights, from the beginning. So the concept has had a very long history. Plato and Aristotle wrestled with the notions of freedom and justice, while Thomas Aquinas and other medieval theologians Christianised the thought of the Greeks in terms of 'natural rights.' Britain looks back gratefully to *Magna Carta*, which King John was induced to sign in 1215, and which King Henry III reissued ten years later. Among its provisions were the guarantees of freedom for the Church and of fair trial by one's peers. Another milestone in British history was the Bill of Rights (1688-9), which made the crown subject to parliament.

America and France look back to their revolutions towards the end of the eighteenth century as the time when constitutional rights were secured for their citizens. The American 'Declaration of Independence' (1776), drafted by Thomas Jefferson, affirmed as 'self-evident' that 'all men are created equal and that they are endowed by their Creator with certain inalienable rights,' especially the rights to 'life, liberty and the pursuit of happiness.' Similar language was used in France's 'Declaration of the Rights of Man and of Citizens,' which was promulgated by its National Assembly in 1789. It speaks of man's 'natural, imprescriptible and unalienable rights' or 'the natural, inalienable and sacred rights of man.' This Declaration was eloquently defended by Thomas Paine in his celebrated book *The Rights of Man* (1791). I shall quote from it presently.

Yet it was World War II, with the horrors of Hitler's savagery and of Japan's brutality, which brought human rights to the top of the world's agenda. In June 1941 President Roosevelt made his famous 'State of the Union' speech, in which he looked forward to the emerging of 'a world founded upon four essential freedoms'—freedom of speech and expression, the freedom of every person to worship God in his own way, freedom from want, and freedom from fear—after each of which he added the words 'everywhere in the world.'[3]

The United Nations organisation was established in 1945. The preamble to its charter reads: 'We, the people of the United Nations,' are determined 'to reaffirm faith in fundamental human rights, in the dignity and worth of the human person, the equal rights of men and women and of nations large and small. . . .' Article 1 speaks of international cooperation 'in promoting and encouraging respect for human rights and for fundamental freedoms for all without distinction as to race, sex, language or religion.' Article 55 goes further and says that the United Nations *shall* promote 'universal respect for, and observance of, human rights and fundamental freedoms for all without distinction as to race, sex, language or religion.'

The following year the United Nations established the 'Human Rights Commission,' under the chairmanship of President Roosevelt's widow, Eleanor, charged with the task of preparing a 'Universal Declaration of Human Rights' as the first element in the international 'Bill of Rights' which it had been commissioned to produce. Its preamble affirms that 'recognition of the inherent dignity, of the equal and inalienable rights, of all members of the human family, is the foundation of freedom, justice and peace in the world. . . .' Article 1 declares that 'all human beings are born free and equal in dignity and rights. . . .' Article 2 adds that 'everyone is entitled to all the rights and freedoms set forth in the Declaration, without distinction of any kind, such as race, colour, sex, language, religion, political or other opinion, national or social origin, property, birth or other status.' The first part of the Declaration covers political and civil rights, and the second part economic, social, and cultural rights. It was adopted by the UN General Assembly in Paris on 10 December 1948, though not all nations ratified it.

Writing of the late 1940s while the draft Declaration was being prepared, Dr. Charles H. Malik, from the Christian community of Lebanon, later to become President of the UN General Assembly, wrote: 'We believed that nothing was more needful in a world that had just emerged from a most devastating war—devastating not only physically, economically, politically, but above all morally, spiritually, humanly—than to recapture and reaffirm the full integrity of man. We loved man and thought him to be wonderful, and we wanted him to be fully himself, enjoying his inherent dignity and freedom, and yet as we looked around, we found only caricatures of humanity—men deprived of their material needs, oppressed by the ideas with which they interpreted themselves and the world, distorted by the arbitrary laws of their governments, warped by the customs and convictions of their societies, diminished and disfigured in their human stature. . . . Therefore we set about inquiring how much . . . we could define and protect what belonged to the essence of man. I never worked harder, I never had a surer sense of self-confidence, I never pulsated with a deeper existential joy, than in those memorable days.'[4]

The adoption of the Universal Declaration was only the beginning. The European Convention for the Protection of Human Rights (1950) was followed by the creation of the European Commission on Human Rights (1953) and of the European Court of Human Rights in 1958. In 1961 Amnesty International was founded. In 1966 the two International Covenants (one on economic, social, and cultural rights, and the other on civil and political rights) were published. The year 1968 was declared the International Year for Human Rights. And in 1973 the Helsinki Conference on Security and Cooperation in Europe was held, whose final 'Act' (1975) included a section on 'The Respect of Human Rights and Fundamental Freedoms.' The following year (1976) the two International Covenants came into effect, and so the long-dreamed-of International Bill of Human Rights became a reality.

This, then, is the paradoxical situation (a Universal Declaration of Human Rights and a widespread violation of them) in which Christians need to ask some basic questions. How is it that human beings have any rights? Whence did they acquire them?

Have Christians anything distinctive to contribute to continuing debate and action about human rights?

It may be good to begin our answers with Thomas Paine. For, although he was a deist and therefore far from being an orthodox Christian, his father was a Quaker and his mother an Anglican, so that he was still Christian enough in his outlook to know that the rights of man go back to the creation of man. He wrote in 1791:

'The error of those who reason by precedents drawn from antiquity, respecting the rights of man, is that they do not go far enough into antiquity. They do not go the whole way. They stop in some of the intermediate stages of an hundred or a thousand years. . . . But if we proceed on, we shall at last come out right; we shall come to the time when man came from the hand of his Maker. What was he then? Man. Man was his high and only title, and a higher cannot be given him.'[5]

Tom Paine was correct. The origin of human rights is creation. Man has never 'acquired' them. Nor has any government or other authority conferred them. Man has had them from the beginning. He received them with his life from the hand of his Maker. They are inherent in his creation. They have been bestowed on him by his Creator.

Put in another way, human rights are the rights of human beings, and the nature of human rights depends on the nature of the human beings, whose rights they are. Animal rights are also important, as considered in chapter six, for God has created them too, although he has not honoured them by stamping his own likeness upon them. Fundamental, therefore, to human rights is the question what it means to be human. Since the Bible focusses on the divine purpose for human beings, it has much to say on this topic. Three words seem to summarise it—*dignity, equality,* and *responsibility.*

Human Dignity

The dignity of human beings is asserted in three successive sentences in Genesis 1.27, 28, which we have already examined in relation to the environment. First, 'God created man in his own image.' Secondly, 'male and female he created them.' Thirdly, 'God blessed them and said to them, ". . . fill the earth and sub-due it." ' Human dignity is here seen to consist of three unique relationships which God established for us by creation, which to-gether constitute a large part of our humanness, and which the Fall distorted but did not destroy.

The first is *our relationship to God.* Human beings are Godlike beings, created by his will in his image. The divine image in-cludes those rational, moral, and spiritual qualities which sepa-rate us from the animals and relate us to God. In consequence, we can learn about him from evangelists or teachers (it is a basic human right to hear the gospel); come to know, love, and serve him; live in conscious, humble dependence upon him; under-stand his will and obey his commands. So then, all those human rights we call the freedom to profess, practice and propagate re-ligion, the freedom of worship, of conscience, of thought, and of speech, come under this first rubric of our relationship to God. It is striking that even the deistic leaders of the American and French revolutions knew this instinctively and referred to the 'Supreme Being' from whom human rights are ultimately derived.

The second unique capacity of human beings concerns *our re-lationship to one another.* The God who made humankind is himself a social being, one God comprising three eternally distinct modes of personhood. He said: 'Let *us* make man in *our* image,' and 'it is not good for the man to be alone.' So God made man male and female, and told them to procreate. Sexuality is his creation, marriage is his institution, and human companionship his purpose. So then, all those human freedoms which we call the sanctity of sex, marriage, and family, the right of peaceful as-sembly, and the right to receive respect, whatever our age, sex, race or rank, come under this second rubric of our relationship to each other.

Our third distinctive quality as human beings is *our relationship to the earth* and its creatures. God has given us dominion, with in-structions to subdue and cultivate the fruitful earth, and rule its creatures. So then, all those human rights we call the right to work and the right to rest, the right to share in the earth's resources, the right to food, clothing, and shelter, the right to life and health, and to their preservation, together with freedom from poverty, hunger, and disease, come under this third rubric of our relationship to the earth.

In spite of the over-simplification, we may sum up what is meant by human dignity in these three ways: our relationship to God (or the right and responsibility of worship), our relationship to each other (or the right and responsibility of fellowship), and our relationship to the earth (or the right and responsibility of stewardship)—together of course with the opportunity which education, income, and health provide to *develop* this unique human potential.

Thus all human rights are at base the right to be human, and so to enjoy the dignity of having been created in God's image and of possessing in consequence unique relationships to God himself, to our fellow human beings, and to the material world. Christians have something important to add to this, namely that our Creator has also redeemed or recreated us, at great personal cost, through the incarnation and atonement of his Son. And the costliness of God's redeeming work reinforces the sense of human worth which his creation had already given us. William Temple expressed this truth with his customary clarity:

'There can be no Rights of Man except on the basis of faith in God. But if God is real, and all men are his sons, that is the true worth of every one of them. My worth is what I am worth to God; and that is a marvellous great deal, for Christ died for me. Thus, incidentally what gives to each of us his highest worth gives the same worth to everyone; in all that matters most we are all equal.'[6]

Our value depends then on God's view of us and relationship to us. As a result of this, human rights are not unlimited rights, as if we were free to be and do absolutely anything we like. They are limited to what is compatible with being the human person God made us and meant us to be. True freedom is found in being our true selves as authentic human beings, not in contradicting ourselves. That is why it has been essential to define 'human being' before defining 'human rights.' This principle will also help to guide us when we come to the demands for 'feminine rights' and 'gay rights.'* The question these demands pose is how far feminism and homosexual practices are compatible with the humanness God has created and intends to safeguard.

In no situation is it permissible to forget the dignity of human beings by creation, and their consequent right to respect. Convicted criminals may justly be deprived of their freedom during a period of imprisonment. But the right to incarcerate does not imply the right to inflict solitary confinement on a prisoner, or to treat him inhumanly in other ways. I was glad to read that Bishop Kurt Scharf of Berlin-Brandenburg visited Ulrike Meinhof and other members of the notorious Baader-Meinhof group in prison, in order to investigate their treatment and listen to their complaints.[7] I am thankful too for the work of Prison Fellowship International founded by Charles Colson after his personal experience of the brutalising effects of incarceration. Inmates, who have been deprived of liberty by a court, may not be deprived of other rights. 'I was in prison,' Jesus said, 'and you visited me.'

Human Equality

The tragedy is that 'human rights' have not always meant 'equal rights.' The good gifts of the Creator are spoiled by human selfishness. The rights God gave to all human beings equally, easily degenerate into *my* rights on which I insist, irrespective of the rights of others or of the common good. So the history of the world has been the story of conflict between my rights and yours, between the good of each and the good of all, between the individual and the community.

Indeed, it is when human rights are in conflict with one another that we are presented with a difficult ethical dilemma. It may be the tension between the rights of the mother and of her

---

* The author discusses 'Sexual Issues' at length in *Involvement, Volume 2.*

unborn child when an abortion is being considered; or between an individual landowner's right to property and peace on the one hand, and the community's need on the other for a new motorway or airport; or between the freedom of speech and assembly which a civil rights group claims for its demonstration and the freedom which the local inhabitants claim not to have their quiet disturbed or their patience provoked.

The conflict of rights regularly envisaged in the Bible, however, takes a rather different form. Its emphasis is that no powerful individual may impose his will on the community, and that no community may violate the rights of an individual or minority. The weak and vulnerable were carefully protected by the Mosaic law. Far from exploiting them, God's people were to be the voice of the voiceless and the champion of the powerless, including their enemies. Paul Oestreicher has put it well:

'When the electrodes are turned on, the torture victim suffers equally when the "security" think they are saving free enterprise from the revolution or the revolution from reaction. . . . My own commitment is neither to liberalism nor to Marxism, but to a curious idea put about by a carpenter turned dissident preacher in Palestine that the test of our humanity is to be found in how we treat our enemies. . . . A society's maturity and humanity will be measured by the degree of dignity it affords to the disaffected and the powerless.'[8]

The equality of human beings is clearly expressed in the familiar Authorised Version words 'no respect of persons.' It is a misleading phrase, because of course persons must at all costs be respected. But what the original Greek expression means literally is 'no acceptance of faces.' In other words, we must show 'no partiality' (NIV) in our attitude to other people, and give no special deference to some because they are rich, famous or influential. The biblical authors insist much on this. Moses declared for example: 'The Lord your God is God of gods and Lord of lords, the great God, mighty and awesome, who shows no partiality . . .' (Deuteronomy 10.17). Therefore Israelite judges were to show no partiality either, but rather give justice 'to the small and to the great alike' (Deuteronomy 1.16, 17; cf. 16.18, 19).

The same emphasis occurs in the New Testament. God is the impartial Judge. He does not regard external appearances or circumstances. He shows no favouritism, whatever our racial or social background may be (e.g. Acts 10.34; Romans 2.11; 1 Peter 1.17). Jesus was once described (perhaps in flattery, but still with accuracy) in these terms: 'Teacher, we know you are a man of integrity. You aren't swayed by men, because you pay no attention to who they are' (Mark 12.14). That is, he neither deferred to the rich and powerful, nor despised the poor and weak, but gave equal respect to all, whatever their social status. We must do the same.

I rather think the best illustration of this principle is to be found in the Book of Job. It is Job's final appeal for justice, after his three comforters have at last stopped their unfair, unkind, untrue accusations. Job clings still to his innocence, while at the same time acknowledging that God is a just judge. If he has broken God's laws (by immorality, idolatry or oppression), then indeed let God's judgment fall upon him. He continues: 'If I have denied justice to my [servants], when they had a grievance against me, what will I do when God confronts me? What will I answer when called to account? Did not he who made me in the womb make them? Did not the same one form us both within our mothers?' (Job 31.13–15). Job continued in a similar vein with reference to the poor and needy, the widows and orphans. We have equal rights because we have the same Creator. Both the dignity and the equality of human beings are traced in Scripture to our creation.

This principle should be even more obvious in the New Testament community, since we have the same Saviour also. Paul regulates the behaviour of masters and slaves to each other by reminding both that they have the same heavenly master, and that 'there is no favouritism with him' (Ephesians 6.9; cf. Colossians 3.25). James seeks to banish class distinctions from public worship by urging that there must be no 'favouritism' between rich and poor among believers in Jesus Christ (James 2.1–9). Yet the same truth is self-evident among unbelievers. Our common humanity is enough to abolish favouritism and privilege, and to establish equal status and rights. All human rights violations contradict the equality we enjoy by creation. 'He who oppresses the poor shows contempt for their Maker' (Proverbs 14.31). If God shows, and if we should show, a 'bias to the poor' (as is now often claimed, and as we shall be considering*), and if such bias is not an infringement of the 'no favouritism' rule, it must be justified either because society as a whole is biassed against them, or because they have no one else to champion them.

The fact that 'there is no favouritism with God' is the foundation of the biblical tradition of prophetic protest. The prophets were courageous in denouncing tyranny in leaders, especially in the kings of Israel and Judah. The fact that they were monarchs, and even 'the Lord's anointed,' did not make them immune to criticism and rebuke. To be sure, due respect was to be shown to rulers because of their office, but any attempts on their part to convert authority into tyranny or rule into despotism, was to be strenuously resisted.

David was the best known of all the kings of Israel, but that gave him no warrant to kill Uriah and steal his wife Bathsheba; God sent the prophet Nathan to rebuke him. When Ahab was king in Samaria, his wife Jezebel thought his power was absolute. 'Do you now govern Israel?' she asked contemptuously, when she found him sulking because Naboth had refused to sell him his vineyard. God sent Elijah to denounce Ahab's later murder of Naboth and seizure of his property. Jehoiakim was King of Judah in the seventh century B.C., yet he had no right to build himself a luxurious palace by forced labour. 'Woe to you,' cried Jeremiah. 'Does it make you a king to have more and more cedar?' The prophet then reminded him of his father Josiah. 'He did what was right and just, so all went well with him. He defended the cause of the poor and needy, and so all went well. . . . But your eyes and your heart are set only on dishonest gain, on shedding innocent blood and on oppression and extortion.' No one would

---

* See note on page 198; the author also treats this subject in that volume.

lament him when he died, Jeremiah added; he would have the burial of a donkey, dragged away and thrown outside the gates of Jerusalem.[9]

In our day dictators try to defend arbitrary arrest and detention, and even imprisonment or execution without public trial, on the ground of 'national security.' One wonders how a biblical prophet would react. Protest or denunciation within the country concerned would doubtless cost the prophet his life. But at least from outside the kind of work which Amnesty International undertakes is consistent with biblical precedent, and with the recognition that with God 'there is no favouritism.' Human rights are equal rights.

Human Responsibility

Christians often cringe when the conversation turns to human rights, for it smacks of one person asserting his rights against another, and so of conflict and selfishness. It is important at this stage, therefore, to clarify the relationship between rights and responsibilities.

The Bible says much about defending other people's rights, but little about defending our own. On the contrary, when it addresses us, it emphasises our responsibilities, not our rights. We are to love God and to love our neighbour. These primary requirements comprise our whole duty; for 'all the Law and the Prophets hang on these two commandments,' Jesus said (Matthew 22.40). In fact, what the Bible contains, as Dr. Christopher Wright has written, is a 'Universal Declaration of Human Responsibilities' (especially in terms of loving God and neighbour), not of human rights.[10] Indeed, the Bible goes further and links them. It emphasises that our responsibility is to secure the other person's rights. We must even forgo our own rights in order to do so.

Of this responsible renunciation of rights Jesus Christ is the supreme model. Although eternally 'in very nature God,' he 'did not consider equality with God something to be grasped, but made himself nothing, taking the very nature of a servant, being made in human likeness' (Philippians 2.6, 7). Throughout his life he was a victim of abuses of human rights. He became a refugee baby in Egypt, a prophet without honour in his own country, and the Messiah rejected by the religious establishment of his own people to whom he had come. He became a prisoner of conscience, refusing to compromise in order to secure his release. He was falsely accused, unjustly condemned, brutally tortured, and finally crucified. And throughout his ordeal he declined to defend or demand his rights, in order that by his self-sacrifice he might serve ours.

'Let this mind be in you, which was also in Christ Jesus,' wrote Paul. And Paul practised what he preached. He had rights as an apostle (the right to marry, the right to receive financial support). But he renounced them for the sake of the gospel, in order to become everybody's slave and so serve their rights (see e.g. 1 Corinthians 9).

The renunciation of rights, however unnatural and idealistic it may seem, is an essential characteristic of God's new society. In the world outside people assert their own rights and exercise authority. 'Not so with you,' Jesus said. On the contrary, in his community those aspiring after greatness must become servants, the leader the slave, and the first last. For love 'is not self-seeking,' Paul wrote. And this fundamental stance, learned from Jesus, applies in every situation. For example, believers should not prosecute one another, especially in an unbelieving court. Christian litigation was a scandal in Corinth; it still is in India, Pakistan, Sri Lanka, and other countries. Christians should at the very least settle their own disputes. Better still, 'why not rather be wronged? Why not rather be cheated?' Is not this the way of Christ?

Another first-century application was to Christian slaves with cruel masters. What if they were unjustly beaten? They must bear it patiently, following in the footsteps of Jesus, who did not retaliate, but entrusted himself and his cause to the Just Judge of all.[11] This last point, that the nonretaliation of Jesus was accompanied by a commitment of himself to God, is an important addition. To renounce rights is not to acquiesce in wrongs. The reason we do not judge is that this is God's prerogative, not ours (Romans 12.19). Besides, Christ is coming back, and then all evil will be judged, and justice finally and publicly vindicated.

Here then is a Christian perspective on human rights. First, we affirm human dignity. Because human beings are created in God's image to know him, serve one another and be stewards of the earth, therefore they must be respected. Secondly, we affirm human equality. Because human beings have all been made in the same image by the same Creator, therefore we must not be obsequious to some and scornful of others, but behave without partiality to all. Thirdly, we affirm human responsibility. Because God has laid it upon us to love and serve our neighbour, therefore we must fight for his rights, while being ready to renounce our own in order to do so.

Two main conclusions follow. First, we have to accept that other people's rights are our responsibility. We *are* our brother's keeper, because God has put us in the same human family and so made us related to and responsible for one another. The law and the prophets, Jesus and his apostles, all lay on us a particular duty to serve the poor and defend the powerless. We cannot escape this by saying they are not our responsibility. As Solzhenitsyn has written, 'there are no internal affairs left on this globe of ours. Mankind can be saved only if everybody takes an interest in everybody else's affairs.'[12] We need then to feel the pain of those who suffer oppression. 'Remember those in prison as if you were their fellow prisoners, and those who are mistreated as if you yourselves were suffering' (Hebrews 13.3). In order to do this, we may need to inform ourselves more thoroughly about contemporary violations of human rights.[13] Then whatever action we may believe it right to take, we need to ensure that the methods we use do not infringe the very human rights we are seeking to champion.

Secondly, we have to take more seriously Christ's intention that the Christian community should set an example to other communities. I am not thinking only of our Christian conduct at home and work, in which as husbands or wives, parents or children, employers or employees we are to be submissive to one another out of reverence for Christ (Ephesians 5.21). I am thinking particularly of the life of the local church, which is meant to be a sign of God's rule. The Church should be the one community in the world in which human dignity and equality are invariably recognised, and human responsibility for each other accepted; the rights of others are sought and never violated, while our own are often renounced; there is no partiality, favouritism or discrimination; the poor and the weak are defended, and human beings are free to be human as God made us and meant us to be.

Notes

Chapter 1

1. *Evangelism and Social Responsibility: An Evangelical Commitment*, The Grand Rapids Report (Exeter: Paternoster 1982), p. 19.
2. J. Wesley Bready, *England: Before and After Wesley* (Sevenoaks: Hodder & Stoughton, 1939), pp. 11, 14.
3. Ibid. p. 126.
4. Ibid. p. 405.
5. Ibid. p. 405.
6. Ibid. p. 327.
7. Ibid. p. 316.
8. Ernest Marshall Howse, *Saints in Politics*, 'the "Clapham Sect" and the growth of freedom' (London: George Allen & Unwin, 1953), p. 26.
9. Ibid. p. 27.
10. Georgina Battiscombe, *Shaftesbury*, a biography of the 7th Earl 1801–1885 (London: Constable, 1974), p. 334.
11. Quoted by David O. Moberg in *The Great Reversal*, 'evangelism versus social concern' (London: Scripture Union 1972, 1973), p. 184. For an account of evangelical social work in Britain in the nineteenth century, see also *Evangelicals in Action* by Kathleen Heasman (Petworth: Geoffrey Bles, 1962).
12. Donald W. Dayton, *Discovering an Evangelical Heritage* (New York: Harper & Row, 1976), pp. 15–24. See also *Revivalism and Social Reform*, 'American Protestantism on the Eve of the Civil War' by Timothy L. Smith (Baltimore: Johns Hopkins University Press, 1980). Dr. Smith begins his Preface by saying that Thomas Paine, if he had visited New York in 1865, would have been amazed to discover that 'the emancipating glory of the great awakenings had made Christian liberty, Christian equality and Christian fraternity the passion of the land' (p. 7).
13. Op. cit. p. 25.
14. From an article by Donald W. Dayton in *The Post-American* (March 1975).
15. From the Introduction by R. Pierce Beaver to *Christian Mission and Social Justice* by Samuel Escobar and John Driver (Scottdale: Herald Press, 1978), pp. 7–9.
16. Walter Rauschenbusch, *Christianity and the Social Crisis* (London: Macmillan, 1907).
17. Ibid. pp. 391–400.
18. Ibid. p. 357.
19. Ibid. p. 65.
20. Ibid. p. xiii.
21. Ibid. p. 149.

22. Ibid. p. 420.

23. Ibid. p. 210.

24. Ibid. p. 380.

25. Walter Rauschenbusch, *A Theology for the Social Gospel* (New York: Macmillan, 1917, 1918).

26. Ibid. p. 1.

27. Ibid. p. 131.

28. Ibid. p. 142.

29. Ibid. p. 145.

30. Op. cit. pp. 53–57.

31. *Keele 67*, the National Evangelical Anglican Congress, ed. Philip Crowe (Eastbourne: Falcon, 1967), para. 20.

32. Op. cit. p. 28.

33. Op. cit. pp. 43, 44.

34. Op. cit. p. 45.

35. Dr. Edward Norman, *Christianity and the World Order* (Oxford University Press, 1979).

36. Tom Sine, *The Mustard Seed Conspiracy* (Waco: Word, 1981), pp. 69–71.

37. John Gladwin, *God's People in God's World*, biblical motives for social involvement (Leicester: IVP, 1979), p. 125.

38. H. J. Blackman, *Humanism* (New York: Penguin, 1968). He writes: 'Humanism is the human case and the human cause, an age-old conviction about the human case. . . . which will induce men and women . . . to espouse the human cause with head and heart and with two hands.' (p. 9).

39. Ed. Sir Julian Huxley, *The Humanist Frame* (London: George Allen & Unwin, 1961), p. 47.

40. Summarised from *The Elephant Man and Other Reminiscences* by Sir Frederick Treves (London: Cassell, 1923). For a thoroughly researched account of the whole affair, see *The True History of the Elephant Man* by Michael Howell and Peter Ford (New York: Penguin, 1980).

41. Quoted by Charles Smyth in *Cyril Forster Garbett* (Sevenoaks: Hodder & Stoughton, 1959), p. 106.

42. A. R. Vidler, *Essays in Liberality* (London: SCM Press, 1957), pp. 95–112. Dr. Vidler contrasted it with 'unholy worldliness' which is 'to conform uncritically and complacently to the standards and fashions that prevail . . .' (p. 96).

43. A. N. Triton, *Whose World?* (Leicester: IVP, 1970), pp. 35–36.

Chapter 2

1. William Temple, *Citizen and Churchman* (London: Eyre & Spottiswoode, 1941), p. 82.

2. Ibid. p. 83.

3. Ibid. p. 84.

4. William Temple, *Christianity and the Social Order* (New York: Penguin, 1942), p. 29.

5. Ibid. p. 31.

6. Harry Blamires, *The Christian Mind* (London: SPCK, 1963), p. 70.

7. Ibid. p. 43.

8. Ibid. p. 3.

9. Ibid. p. 50.

10. Theodore Roszak, *Where the Wasteland Ends*, 'Politics and Transcendence in Post-industrial Society' (New York: Anchor 1972, 1973), pp. xxi and 67.

11. J. S. Whale *Christian Doctrine* (London: J. M. Fontana, 1941, 1957), p. 33.

12. Reinhold Niebuhr, *The Children of Light and the Children of Darkness* (Digswell Place: Nisbet, 1945), p. vi.

13. Tom Sine, *The Mustard Seed Conspiracy* (Waco: Word, 1981), p. 70.

14. William Temple, *Christianity and the Social Order* (New York: Penguin, 1942), p. 54.

15. *The Lausanne Covenant*, para. 15. See *The Lausanne Covenant—An Exposition and Commentary* by John Stott (Lausanne Occasional Paper No. 3, published by the Lausanne Committee for World Evangelisation, 1975), pp. 33–36.

16. Quoted by Stuart Barton Babbage in *The Mark of Cain* (Grand Rapids: Eerdmans, 1966), pp. 17, 18.

17. From *The Essence of Security*, quoted by Gavin Reid in *The Elaborate Funeral* (Sevenoaks: Hodder & Stoughton, 1972), p. 48.

18. J. S. Whale, op. cit., p. 41.

19. Psalms 32.9; 1 Corinthians 14.20.

Chapter 3

1. Chapter 3 in *Essays in Evangelical Social Ethics*, ed. David F. Wright (Exeter: Paternoster, 1978), pp. 59–81.

2. *Attitudes to Bible God Church*, a Research Report by Jan Harrison (Swindon: Bible Society, 1983). The 1983 U.K. Christian Handbook calculates adult church membership as 17.4 percent of the population.

3. *U.K. Christian Handbook 1983 Edition*, ed. Peter Brierley Table 12[A], 13[A].

4. John Kobler, *Ardent Spirits*, 'the rise and fall of prohibition' (London: Michael Joseph, 1974), pp. 216–7.

5. Richard Gutteridge, *Open Thy Mouth for the Dumb*, 'the German Evangelical Church and the Jews 1870–1950' (Oxford: Basil Blackwell, 1976).

6. Ibid. p. 48.

7. Ibid. p. 128.

8. Ibid. p. 181.

9. Ibid. p. 268.

10. Ibid. p. 298.

11. Ibid. p. 299.

12. Ibid. p. 304.

13. O. R. Johnston, *Who Needs the Family?*, 'a survey and a Christian assessment' (Sevenoaks: Hodder & Stoughton, 1979), pp. 43–46.

14. J. D. Unwin, *Sex and Culture* (Oxford University Press, 1934), pp. 411–412 and 431–432.

15. See, for example *Sex and Society* by Hugh Arthur (Presbyterian Church of England, 1969): 'There is no doubt, physiologically and psychologically speaking, that whereas for men intercourse is a pleasure and an end in itself—it is a pleasure and a beginning for a woman. . . . The basic feminine sexual need really is security.'

16. William Temple, *Christianity and the Social Order* (New York: Penguin, 1942), p. 59.

17. Reinhold Niebuhr, *Moral Man and Immoral Society* (New York: Scribner's, 1932, revised edition 1960), pp. xi and xx.

18. John R. Lucas *Democracy and Participation* (London: Pelican, 1975, 1976), p. 10. Also recommended is *The Children of Light and the Children of Darkness* by Reinhold Niebuhr (Digswell Place: Nisbet, 1945). He wrote it eighteen months before the end of World War II, in which he saw 'bourgeois civilization' collapsing before the onslaught of Nazi barbarism, and subtitled his book 'a vindication of democracy and a critique of its traditional defenders.' His faith in democracy was not the blind optimism of liberals who, having no conception of original sin, held a 'fatuous and superficial view of man' (p. 15). It was rather that democracy is the best way to resolve the tension between the individual and the community, self-interest and the common good, freedom and order.

19. John V. Taylor, *Enough is Enough* (London: SCM Press, 1975), pp. 64 and 114.

Chapter 4

1. From his Inaugural Address to students on 28th April, 1972, when installed as Rector of Glasgow University.

2. K. S. Latourette, *History of the Expansion of Christianity*, in seven volumes (London: Eyre & Spottiswoode, 1945), Vol. 7, pp. 503–4.

3. Nikolai Berdyaev, *The Destiny of Man* (Petworth: Geoffrey Bles, 1937), p. 281.

4. William Temple, *Christianity and the Social Order* (New York: Penguin 1942), p. 27.

5. *Christianity Today*, 21st December, 1979.

6. Tom Sine, *The Mustard Seed Conspiracy* (Waco: Word, 1981), p. 113.

7. Matthew 5–7. See my exposition of the Sermon on the Mount, entitled *Christian Counter-Culture* (Leicester: IVP 1978).

8. *Evangelism and Social Responsibility: An Evangelical Commitment*, the Grand Rapids Report (published 1982 by Paternoster Press on behalf of the Lausanne Committee for World Evangelisation, and the Worldwide Evangelical Fellowship), p. 49.

9. Ibid. p. 23.

10. Ibid. p. 24.

11. Brian Griffiths, *Morality and the Market Place*, 'Christian Alternatives to Capitalism and Socialism' (Sevenoaks: Hodder & Stoughton, 1982), p. 69.

12. *North-South*, 'A Programme for Survival,' the Report of the Independent Commission on International Development Issues under the chairmanship of Willy Brandt (London: Pan Books, 1980), p. 25.

13. *Morality and the Market Place*, pp. 148–9.

14. Ibid. pp. 154–5.

15. Alexander Solzhenitsyn, *One Word of Truth* (London: Bodley Head, 1972), pp. 22–7.

16. Speech by Sir Keith Joseph in Birmingham in October, 1974.

17. John Howard Yoder, *The Politics of Jesus* (Grand Rapids: Eerdmans, 1972), pp. 111 and 157.

18. *Evangelism and Social Responsibility: An Evangelical Commitment* (1982), p. 34.

19. Dom Helder Camara, *Spiral of Violence* (London: Sheed & Ward, 1970, 1971), p. 69.

20. Dom Helder Camara, *The Desert is Fertile* (London: Sheed & Ward, 1974), p. 3.

21. *Spiral of Violence*, p. 43.

22. Dom Helder Camara, *Race Against Time* (London: Sheed & Ward, 1971), pp. vii–viii.

23. Ibid. p. 17.

24. Tom Sine, *The Mustard Seed Conspiracy* (Waco: Word, 1981), pp. 11–12.

Chapter 5

1. Albert Einstein, in a telegram asking prominent persons for funds for the Atomic Scientists' Emergency Committee, cited in the *New York Times*, 25 May 1946.

2. For these statistics see *The Military Balance 1983–84* (International Institute for Strategic Studies 1983), pp. 118, 125–6. Also *World Armaments and Disarmament* (SIPRI Yearbook 1983).

3. *Common Security: A Programme for Disarmament*, the Palme Commission Report (London: Pan Books 1982), p. 2; cf. also p. 71. See also *The Military Balance 1983–84*, pp. 125–128.

4. From an address entitled 'The Chance for Peace' and delivered on 16 April 1953. *Public Papers of the Presidents of the United States: Dwight Eisenhower, 1953* (Washington: US Government Printing Office, 1960), p. 182.

5. Jim Wallis, ed., *Waging Peace*, 'A Handbook for the Struggle to Abolish Nuclear Weapons' (New York: Harper & Row, 1982), p. 44.

6. From Earl Mountbatten's 'The Final Abyss?' speech in May 1979, published in *Apocalypse Now?* (Nottingham: Spokesman Books, 1980), p. 11.

7. See also *The Long-Term Biological Consequences of Nuclear War* (1983), the report of an international conference sponsored by thirty-one groups. Two imaginative scenarios, written by military men, were published in 1978. *World War 3*, edited by Brigadier Shelford Bidwell (Feltham: Hamlyn, 1978), 'a military projection founded on today's facts,' predicted that in 1983 the third world war would start 'as the result of some intolerable provocation' (p. xiii), e.g. the invasion of West Germany by Soviet tanks to prevent her becoming a nuclear power. The last chapter is entitled 'Doomsday' and describes the final, total devastation. *The Third World War* by General Sir John Hackett, assisted by top-ranking American and German generals (London: Sidgwick & Jackson, 1978), calls itself 'a future history.' It also describes an invasion of West Germany by Soviet tanks, though in 1985, which steadily escalates until first Birmingham and then in retaliation Minsk are obliterated by nuclear missiles. This time, however, the final holocaust is averted by the uprising against the Soviet Union of her satellites.

The ghastly consequences of a nuclear explosion are factually described by

Donald B. Kraybill in *Facing Nuclear War* (Scottdale: Herald Press, 1982) and in *Common Security* (the Palme Commission report, 1982), pp. 49–70.

8. For recent statements of the pacifist position see *Christ and Violence* by Ronald J. Sider (Kitchener: Herald Press, Canada, 1979) and *Nuclear Holocaust and Christian Hope* by Ronald J. Sider and Richard K. Taylor (Downers Grove: InterVarsity, 1982).

9. The theory of the 'just war' is carefully argued in two books by Paul Ramsey: *War and the Christian Conscience* (Durham: Duke University Press, 1961) and *The Just War* (New York: Scribners, 1968). For more recent statements of the 'just war' position see Arthur F. Holmes in *War: Four Christian Views* (Downers Grove: InterVarsity, 1981), pp. 120–1; *The Church and the Bomb* (London: Hodder, 1982), pp. 82–98; and *The Challenge of Peace: God's Promise and Our Response*, The U.S. Bishops' Pastoral Letter (CTS/SPCK, 1983), p. 24–32. For a similar position based on the justice of God see *Peace and Justice in the Nuclear Age* by Jerram Barrs (Garamond Press, 1983).

10. Dale Aukerman, *Darkening Valley*, 'a biblical perspective on nuclear war' (New York: Seabury, 1981), ch. 15, p. 95.

11. Ibid. pp. 92–4.

12. It needs to be added that in some emergency situations when no policeman is present, it may be right for a citizen to intervene in a fight, protect an innocent person against assault, or arrest a burglar. But in such cases the citizen is temporarily constituting himself an arm of the law; he is not acting as a private individual, nor is he justified in feeling personal animosity or taking personal revenge.

13. Oliver O'Donovan, *In Pursuit of a Christian View of War*, Grove Booklet on Ethics No. 15 (Bramcote: Grove Books, 1977), pp. 13–14. This booklet is a valuable enquiry into the legitimacy of the analogy between domestic justice and warfare.

14. *Pastoral Constitution*, paragraph 80.

15. E.g. Genesis 9.4; Leviticus 17.11; Deuteronomy 12.23.

16. *The Church and the Atom*, the report of a Church of England Commission (1948), p. 43. For a factual account of the bombing of German and Japanese cities see *The Almanac of World War II*, Brigadier Peter Young, ed. (Feltham: Hamlyn, 1981). Bishop Bell's speech in the House of Lords is recorded in *Hansard* (9th Feb. 1944), vol. 130, pp. 738–46. It is also referred to in *George Bell, Bishop of Chichester* by Ronald C. D. Jasper (Oxford University Press, 1967), pp. 276–77.

17. *Gaudium et Specs* ('The Church in the Modern World'), paragraph 80, 1965, in *The Documents of Vatican II*, W. M. Abbot and J. Gallagher, eds. (London-Dublin: Geoffrey Chapman, 1966).

18. British Council of Churches resolution.

19. *The Church and the Bomb*, 'nuclear weapons and Christian conscience,' an unofficial report of a Church of England working party (Sevenoaks: Hodder & Stoughton, 1982), p. 97.

20. Ibid. pp. 143–4.

21. Ibid. p. 162.

22. 'The New Abolitionist Covenant' is printed on pp. 17–21 of *Waging Peace*, 'a handbook for the struggle to abolish nuclear weapons.' See also *Peace-Makers*, 'Christian Voices from the New Abolitionist Movement,' Jim Wallis, ed. (New York: Harper & Row, 1983).

23. Michael Quinlan, 'The Meaning of Deterrence' in *The Cross and the Bomb*, Francis Bridges, ed. (Oxford: Mowbrays, 1983), p. 143.

24. *The Challenge of Peace. See* note 9, pp. 43–46.

25. *Before It's Too Late*, 'The Challenge of Nuclear Disarmament,' Paul Abrecht and Ninan Koshy, eds. (WCC, 1983), p. 10.

26. Hugh Beach, 'Where Does the Nuclear-Free Path Lead?' in *The Cross and the Bomb*, op. cit. p. 126.

27. Earl Mountbatten of Burma in *Apocalypse Now?* (Nottingham: Spokesman, 1980), pp. 10, 12.

28. Roger Ruston, O. P., *Nuclear Deterrence–Right or Wrong?* A study prepared for the Roman Catholic Commission for International Justice and Peace (Catholic Information Services, 1981), pp. 35–36, 58.

29. *Common Security*, the Palme Commission Report (1982), p. 105.

30. Ibid. pp. 141, 149.

31. *See*, e.g. *Nuclear Weapons and Christian Conscience*, Walter Stein, ed. (London: Merlin Press, 1961, 1980) and *Ethics and Nuclear Deterrence*, Geoffrey Goodwin, ed. (Beckenham: Croom Helm, 1982).

32. *The Apocalyptic Premise: Nuclear Arms Debated*, Ernest Lefever and Stephen Hunt, eds. (Ethics and Public Policy Center, Washington DC, 1982), pp. 351–9.

33. *The Cross and the Bomb*, 'Christian Ethics and the Nuclear Debate,' Francis Bridger, ed. (Oxford: Mowbray, 1983), pp. 50, 60, 64–5.

34. From an article in *The Guardian Weekly* on 4th April, 1982.

35. Robert W. Gardiner, *The Cool Arm of Destruction* (Philadelphia: Westminster, 1974), quoted by Robert G. Clouse in *War: Four Christian Views*, pp. 193–4.

36. From Dr. David Owen's Introduction to the Palme Commission Report (1982), p. xxi.

37. *Evangelism and Social Responsibility: An Evangelical Commitment* (Exeter: Paternoster, 1982), p. 49.

38. *The Church and the Bomb*, p. 21.

39. From an article entitled 'The Peace Movement and the Soviet Union' (1982), republished in *Who is For Peace?* by Francis Schaeffer, Vladimir Bukovsky, and James Hitchcock (Nashville: Thomas Nelson, 1983), pp. 72–73.

40. *See*, for example, *Defence Without the Bomb*, the Report of the Alternative Defence Commission (Taylor and Francis, 1983).

41. *Common Security*, the report of the Palme Commission, pp. ix, 4, and 100.

42. Ibid. pp. 8–10 and pp. 138–140.

Chapter 6

1. E. F. Schumacher, *Small is Beautiful* (London: Abacus, 1973, 1974), pp. 11–16.

2. *Futures*, vol. v, no. 1 (February 1973), published by I. P. C. Business Press.

3. Gerhard von Rad, *Genesis* (1956; SCM 1963), p. 58.

4. Tom Dale and Vernon Gill Carter, *Topsoil and Civilisation* (1955), quoted by E. F. Schumacher in *Small is Beautiful* (London: Abacus, 1973, 1974), p. 84.

5. Martin Hengel, *Property and Riches in the Early Church* (Philadelphia: Fortress, 1973; SCM, 1974), p. 12.

6. *Laborem Exercens*, Pope John Paul II's Encyclical Letter on 'Human Work' (Catholic Truth Society, 1981), pp. 50–51.

7. Ron Elsdon, *Bent World,* Science, the Bible and the environment (London: Inter Varsity Press, 1981), pp. 20–21.

8. I have culled these facts and figures from various sources, e.g. *The Question Mark,* 'The End of Homo Sapiens,' by Hugh Montefiore (London: Collins, 1969), pp. 15–40, and *Ecology Crisis* 'God's Creation and Man's Pollution,' by John W. Klotz (St. Louis: Concordia, 1972), pp. 9–43.

9. Rowland Moss, *The Earth in Our Hands* (London: Inter Varsity Press, 1982), p. 109.

10. *Man In His Living Environment,* 'An Ethical Assessment,' a report of the Board for Social Responsibility (Church Information Office, 1970), p. 61.

11. Gavin Maxwell's article appeared in *The Observer* on 13 October, 1963.

12. C. F. D. Moule, *Man and Nature in the New Testament,* 'Some Reflections on Biblical Ecology' (London: Athlone, 1964; Philadelphia: Fortress, 1967), p. 1.

13. From an article, 'The Historical Roots of our Ecological Crisis,' in *Science* 155 (1967), pp. 1203–7. It began as an address to the American Association for the Advancement of Science and has been reprinted by (among others) Francis Schaeffer in *Pollution and the Death of Man* (Sevenoaks: Hodder & Stoughton, 1970).

14. Ian L. McHarg, *Design with Nature* (New York: Doubleday, 1969), p. 26.

15. Ibid. p. 197.

16. These extracts from Ian McHarg's Dunning Trust Lectures were quoted in the *Ontario Naturalist,* March 1973.

17. Barbara Ward and René Dubos, *Only One Earth,* 'The Care and Maintenance of a Small Planet' (New York: Penguin, 1972), p. 83.

18. Op. cit. p. 45.

19. Op. cit. p. 85.

20. *Man in His Living Environment,* p. 36.

21. Ronald Higgins, *The Seventh Enemy* (1978).

22. Klaus Bockmühl, *Conservation and Lifestyle* (1975, translated by Bruce N. Kaye. Bramcote: Grove Books 1977), pp. 23–24.

23. Ronald Higgins, ibid. p. 5.

Chapter 7

1. *North-South: A Programme for Survival,* the Report of the Independent Commission on International Development Issues under the chairmanship of Willy Brandt (London: Pan Books, 1980), pp. 7, 8.

2. Ibid. p. 105.

3. Ibid. p. 50.

4. Ibid. p. 32.

5. Brandt Commission, *Common Crisis,* 'North-South: Cooperation for World Recovery' (London: Pan Books, 1983), pp. 9, 10.

6. Ibid. p. 23.

7. Ibid. p. 49.

8. Ibid. pp. 276–280.

9. Ibid. p. 64.

10. Ibid. p. 64.

11. Ibid. p. 30.

12. Brian Griffiths, *Morality and the Market Place*, 'Christian Alternatives to Capitalism and Socialism' (Sevenoaks: Hodder & Stoughton, 1982), p. 127.

13. *North-South*, op. cit. p. 63.

14. *North-South*, op. cit. p. 25.

15. *Moralilty and the Market Place*, p. 143.

16. Ibid. pp. 148, 9.

17. *The Year 2000 AD*, ed. John Stott (Basingstoke: Marshall, Morgan & Scott, 1983), pp. 72–102.

18. Ibid. pp. 92, 3.

19. Ibid. p. 94.

20. Ibid. p. 95.

21. *North-South*, p. 265.

22. Brandt Commission, *Common Crisis*.

23. Ibid. p. 1.

24. Barbara Ward and René Dubos, *Only One Earth*, 'the care and maintenance of a small planet,' an unofficial report commissioned by the Secretary General of the United Nations Conference on the Human Environment, prepared with the assistance of a 152-member Committee of Corresponding Consultants in 58 countries (London: Penguin, 1972).

25. Op. cit. p. 298.

26. Duncan Munro, *Trade, Justice and the Wealth of Nations* (Bramcote: Grove Books, 1976), pp. 11 and 24.

27. Barbara Ward, *Progress for a Small Planet* (London: Penguin, 1979), p. 277.

28. Ibid. p. 257.

29. Roger D. Hansen and others, *US Foreign Policy and the Third World: Agenda 1982* (Eastbourne: Praeger, 1982), p. 234.

30. For the same Spirit, *see* e.g. Romans 8.9 and 1 Corinthians 12.13. For different spiritual gifts, *see* e.g. Romans 12.3–8 and 1 Corinthians 12.4–31.

31. *Gospel and Culture*, the Willowbank Report (Lausanne Occasional Paper No. 2, London: Scripture Union, 1978), p. 29.

32. From a 1967 speech on the Arusha Declaration, published in *Freedom and Socialism, uhuru na ujamaa*, a selection from the writings and speeches of Julius Nyerere 1965-1967 (Oxford University Press, Dar-es-Salaam, 1968), p. 326.

33. Brandt Commission Report, p. 58.

34. Ibid. p. 30.

Chapter 8

1. It is difficult to obtain accurate statistics of human rights violations. I have culled mine from a variety of sources including Amnesty International's annual reports and David Hayes' book *Human Rights* (Hove: Wayland, 1980).

2. From the Editorial by Emilio Castro in *International Review of Mission*, vol. LXVI No. 263, devoted to 'Human Rights' (July 1977), p. 218.

3. The most handy collection of texts is *Basic Documents on Human Rights*, edited by Ian Brownlie (Oxford: Clarendon, second edition, 1981).

4. From Dr. Malik's Introduction to *Free and Equal*, 'human rights in ecumenical perspective,' by O. Frederick Nolde (Geneva: World Council of Churches, 1968), p. 7.

5. Thomas Paine, *The Rights of Man* (1791), eighth edition, pp. 47, 48.

6. William Temple, *Citizen and Churchman* (London: Eyre & Spottiswoode, 1941), pp. 74, 75.

7. See 'The Human Rights of the Malefactor' by Bishop Kurt Scharf in *International Review of Mission*, op. cit. pp. 231–9.

8. Paul Oestreicher, *Thirty Years of Human Rights* (the British Churches' Advisory Forum On Human Rights, 1980).

9. The prophetic protest against these three kings is found in 2 Samuel 11, 12 (Nathan and David), 1 Kings 21 (Elijah and Ahab), and Jeremiah 22.13–19 (Jeremiah and Jehoiakim).

10. Christopher J. H. Wright, *Human Rights: A Study in Biblical Themes* (Grove Booklet on Ethics, No. 31, 1979), p. 16.

11. For this renunciation of rights see Mark 10.42–45 ('not so with you'); 1 Corinthians 13.5 (love); 1 Corinthians 6.1–8 (litigation), and 1 Peter 2.18–25 (slaves).

12. Nobel Prize speech, 1970.

13. Accurate, up-to-date information about the situation in the Soviet Union and Eastern Europe, based on conscientious research, is available from Keston College, which is the Institute for the Study of Religion and Communism, Heathfield Road, Keston, Kent BR2, 6BA, in Great Britain. For information about human rights violations in general, and about imprisonment and torture in particular, write to Amnesty International, 304 W. 58th St., New York, NY 10019; in England, Tower House, Southampton Street, London WC2.

Index

217